'BEST'
OF BOTH
WORLDS

A Tribute
to a Great Medium

Rosalind Cattenach

First published 1999 Pembridge Publishing
ISBN 0953481603

This edition 2016
Saturday Night Press Publications
England

snppbooks@gmail.com
www.snppbooks.com

ISBN 978 1 908421 26 5

printed by Lightning Source
www.lightningsource.com

www.snppbooks.com

Contents

Publisher's Note:

Please be aware, although time has passed, we have presented the book as it was first published in 1999 with the exception of the illustrations which are no longer glossy inclusions but set within the text.

Although Lynn de Swarte is not now Editor of 'Psychic News' we see no reason to change this Acknowledgement in this edition.

We sincerely hope you will enjoy reading of this wonderful medium who brought joy and hope to so many. Ann Harrison

Acknowledgements

I wish to express my sincere thanks to Professor Archie Roy of Glasgow University for writing the foreword to this book and allowing me to quote from his book *A Sense of Something Strange*.

I should also like to thank Linda Rowan for her guidance and Lyn de Swarte, Editor of *Psychic News* for allowing me to examine the many press cuttings pertaining to Albert's spiritual work. My gratitude to Don Galloway and Tony Ortzen for their valuable advice, and all those friends who have contributed to this book.

Foreword

I am glad to have been asked to write an introduction to this book of memories of and testimonials to Albert Best. It is my great fortune to have known him for many years and so I feel it a privilege to have the opportunity to write these words and try to convey to the reader the high value I put on his mediumship and on his friendship.

It was John Macdonald, Professor of Hebrew and Semitic languages in the University of Glasgow, who, knowing of my long term interest in psychical research, first took me to Albert's house to meet him. That first meeting, and a subsequent one, are described elsewhere in this book. It is sufficient to say here that I latterly became convinced that I was in the presence of a man with a powerful psychic faculty. As I got to know him better and our friendship grew, and as I watched him many times demonstrate from the platform of Berkeley St church and elsewhere, my conviction deepened that Albert's mediumship was of superstar quality. Whereas it is well known that many genuine mediums exhibit difficulty in grasping names, Albert would not only give relevant names quickly and clearly but also provide addresses to go with them. When I got to know him better and learned the interesting fact that in his earlier life he had been a postman, accustomed to associating names and addresses for many years, I entertained the possibility that his psychic gift utilised his years of conditioning as a postman. There would be no 'fishing'; out would come the names and addresses, to the consternation of the recipients.

Many sceptics, who presumably have never sat with someone like Albert, will claim that his ostensible 'hits'were guesswork, or cold reading, that is, the sneaky gathering of information from the appearance and response of the recipient. to be worked on and then trotted out as facts fed from 'spirit'. To myself and those others who studied Albert's psychic abilities, such an 'explanation' is laughably inadequate.Facts, incidents. names. addresses were delivered with confidence before the recipient had even uttered a word. At the very least, it was a demonstration of paranormally acquired information.

For many years as a psychical researcher investigating spontaneous cases I was able to depend upon Albert's help. From 1994 on, the Rev Max Magee, Chaplain to the University of Strathclyde students, and I would be called out at times to help families who correctly or incorrectly believed themselves to be the victim of paranormal forces. When we felt that a particular case had possibly paranormal overtones, we would take Albert to the location to see what he could detect. We made a rule of never telling Albert anything of the case, not even which town we were going to. It was astonishing when we got to the location how often he was able to describe in detail the situation. One such case is described later in this book (chapter 7; Built-in with the Bricks). We learned to rely on Albert's kindness, his wish to help and the use of his psychic gift. In later years after Max left Glasgow and I was fortunate after a time to enlist the help of Mrs Trish Robertson of the Scottish Society for Psychical Research, Trish and I were given similar unstinting help by Albert in cases we encountered.

And so over the years my knowledge of and friendship with Albert Best developed. And over the years I learned from others in how many different ways he used his mediumship to help the afflicted and the heartbroken of the world. In the exercise of his mediumship he brought a lightening of the crushing load of bereavement to many people.

Nonetheless he was a difficult man to get to know well for he had a natural shyness and reticence about himself. He could be irritating too when he brushed aside suggestions that his biography should be written, smiling in genuine modesty at the thought that it would be of value. "Maybe someday," he would say to us, "but not yet." He could also be irritating to his many close friends by his carelessness in looking after himself. But some of us, knowing the tragic and crushing blow delivered to him when he was a young man, thought we knew why. As a young soldier in the second World War he returned home to Belfast to be given the shattering news that his wife and children had been killed in the Belfast blitz. Many of us sensed that as a consequence his long journey through this life was essentially a lonely walk towards the day when he believed he would be reunited with them.

I can never think of Albert and the loss of his wife Rose and his children without thinking also of Arthur James Balfour, Prime Minister and president of the Society for Psychical Research, who in 1875 as a young man lost suddenly Mary Catherine Lyttelton, the girl he loved and wished to marry. Like Albert, he too never married. To a friend whose son was killed in the first World War, he wrote: "For myself I entertain no doubt whatever about a future life. I deem it at least as certain as any of the hundred and one truths of the framework of the world ... it is no mere theological accretion, which I am prepared to accept in some moods and reject in others. The bitterness lies not in the thought that those I love and have lost are really dead, still less in the thought that I have parted with them for ever: for I think neither of these things. The bitterness lies in the thought that until I also die I shall never again see them smile or hear their voices. The pain is indeed hard to bear; too hard it sometimes seems for human strength. Yet, measured on the true scale of things it is brief; death cannot long cheat us of love." Those words, I believe give an insight into Albert's behaviour and attitude to life. Happy to be with his friends, glad to use his mediumship to help those in need, he still always maintained that certain reticence.

In this post-religious age many people, believing the materialist's claim that it has been proved scientifically that death is the end, have stoically resigned themselves to the bleak prospect of extinction when they die or accepted that they will never see their loved ones again. Sadly, such people do not appreciate that the study of genuine and gifted mediums like Albert Best by psychical researchers over the past century has at the very least shown conclusively that there is a part of a human being that can operate outwith the bounds of time and space and probably mortality itself.

Albert has gone now. His life as a medium, healer, psychic detective is over. Like many who knew him, I have lost a friend I held in high regard. And so I am glad that this book, a tribute put together from many people's memories, will hopefully let others who never met him realise why we who knew Albert consider him simply to have been "The Best".

Archie E Roy
August 1998

1
Entrance

Albert Best was born in Belfast on 2nd December 1917, and very little is known of his early years. Albert was a very private person and it was understood that his mother died when he was an infant and he was brought up by a Mrs Best whom he believed to be his grandmother. It was not a happy childhood and he never wished to dwell upon this or discuss it. When he finally agreed to a short biography being written I promised to respect his wishes. The important fact is that this great soul entered the earth plane on 2nd December 1917. Mrs Best had four adult daughters whom Albert regarded as his sisters. They were a strong Protestant family and it was a hard and frugal life. The sisters married and went away to set up their own homes, and Mrs Best was left to bring Albert up by herself.

Albert never forgot his first contact with the paranormal. He was about seven years of age, going up the stairs to bed when he saw a man with a lamp standing above him with string tied around his knees. When he pointed him out to the woman he called his grandmother she told him "You were eating cheese tonight!" But he heard her saying clearly "Father go away, you're frightening the boy." He would never be frightened again although he was to see and hear many things.

Albert was in his teens before he encountered someone who claimed to see spirits. The man was a window cleaner, and he invited Albert along to his Church, where a Medium told him that one day he would wear a uniform and go to Africa, but at that time the prospect of going to England, far less to Africa, seemed remote and the absurdity of it made him laugh.

He was fourteen when he left school and found a job in the ropeworks. By this time Mrs Best had died and there seemed to be no one to whom he could turn, but he heard a voice constantly telling him what to do and what to avoid. He often took walks in the country, frightened to death that someone would hear what he was hearing, in case they thought he was mad or evil, but the voice, which was quite audible at times, was comforting and Albert felt he was being protected. One of his sisters had moved to Irvine in Scotland and Albert joined her for a while. When he returned to Belfast he attended a Spiritualist Church in Chichester with another sister. The Medium at the Church, a Mrs Hill, told Albert he had powers, she could see lights around him, and that he had a Guide. He was invited to sit in a development circle with his window cleaner friend, and others in that circle claimed they could see lights around him.

One Saturday night Albert was standing in a queue for the Empire Theatre in Belfast when he met a girl named Rose Lavery who worked in a Mill and was a Catholic. It was a real love match and in spite of great opposition because of the difference in religious beliefs, he and Rose were married in St Ann's Cathedral, Belfast. There were no relatives present, and someone off the street was asked to be Albert's best man.

When war was declared in September 1939 Albert was called up to the Inniskillin Fusiliers. Rose remained with her family in the New Lodge area of Belfast when Albert was sent with the 6th Battalion of the Inniskillins, part of a newly formed First Army, to assist General Alexander's offensive in Africa where the Eighth Army was pushing Rommel through the Sahara Desert towards Tunis.

The 6th Battalion, with Albert Best among them, arrived in Algiers in November 1940. There was a coastal road to Tunis, the final objective, but the First Army was to take a longer, far harder route, concentrating at Bone on the Algerian coast, then moving inland to take up a line commanding the valley of the Merjerda river, the back door to Tunis.

The steep ridged terrain was lethal, with bombing and machine gun attacks, and the Herman Goering crack enemy division was present with powerful air support. Rain churned the plains into quagmires and the going was hard for the Inniskillins, some of the Arabs they encountered being German spies.

The first task the Inniskillins had to perform was to clear the Goubellet Plain of enemy posts. This was a no-man's-land between a ridge on the north towards Tunis, held by the Allies, and a ridge on the south in the grip of the Germans. When Albert heard the name Goubellet he remembered something that had been said to him by his real grandmother whom he met for the first and last time when he was around the age of fourteen. He had been so overawed that he hadn't said a word as she told him, "You'll be a widower before you are twenty-four. I haven't seen you all my life, but I'll be with you in Goubellet." Rose was at home in Belfast with their three children, and Albert thought of them constantly as he hid up during the day in farmhouses and at night crawled out on missions.

He was wounded and left for burial with eight corpses, but a voice told him to "get up" which he did, and he walked away to the horror of the Germans. He was captured and spent time in a prisoner of war camp, but afterwards would never talk of his experiences as he could not bear to recall the horror of the treatment he received. He finally came home in a hospital ship, the Oxfordshire, but when he reached England a Padre came to him and told him he had no family left. Albert had wondered why he had received no letters from his wife but was told that the mail was not getting through.

Rose and her family had been killed in a terrible bombing raid on Belfast when over a thousand people were wiped out. Albert was devastated. His grandmother's prediction had indeed proved to be true and he never really recovered from this tragedy. For the remainder of his life he grieved for his beloved Rose and children, but he erected a wall around himself and contained this grief, rarely speaking of his loss even to his friends. Already a very caring man, this terrible happening engendered a deep compassion for all others who also had suffered.

Albert spoke very little of his war experiences, but we know that he also fought in Italy, was wounded quite severely on two occasions, being shot through the mouth and also receiving a bad injury to his left hand which left it paralysed.

He was invalided out of the Army some time in 1943 and his war pension for injuries received commenced in June 1945.

2
Mediumistic Beginnings

Miss Strachan, former Secretary of the Kilmarnock Spiritualist Church. relates the following memories of Albert:

When Albert Best first arrived in Scotland in 1944 he settled in Irvine in Ayrshire and lodged with a lady called Mrs McAdam. He worked in the postal service at the time and shared his lodgings with other postal workers.

His first development circle was run by a man called Mr Parks, but he did not stay very long with this group, probably not more than two years. By 1951 Albert had commenced attending the Kilmarnock Spiritualist Church, and one of Albert's fondest memories from this time was the gift from John Findlay of a copy of *In Tune with the Infinite* by Ralph Waldo Trine. This was something he treasured as he loved the book and called it his Bible. Albert was then sitting in a circle with Miss Sims. and in 1955 he served the Kilmarnock Church for the first time, having had his mediumship assessed by Miss Strachan. Miss Strachan remembers Albert as being very shy and never speaking much about his life in Belfast, and she also remembers that Albert's clairvoyant abilities were extraordinary.

To the best of her knowledge Miss Strachan believes that Albert continued his development with Miss Sims until the mid-fifties and shortly after this she thinks he was introduced to Maurice Barbanell, the Editor of *Psychic News*, who helped him to work further afield.

The Testimony of Laurence Goss

Laurence Goss was a friend of Albert Best and was first

introduced to him in 1950 by Miss Sims, the leader of a Spiritualist Circle in Saltcoats, Ayrshire. Albert came to Irvine in 1943 and he sat in a circle there for seven years to develop his spiritual gifts. During this time Albert told of an experience of spiritual phenomena which made him very uncomfortable. Albert told Laurence that whilst resting in his sister's home, where he was then living, he opened his eyes and noticed that ectoplasm was forming and being expelled from his nostrils, mouth and ears, and at this point he called out to the Spirit world "No, no, I don't want this." Albert says after this he was never used in this way again by Spirit. It was the belief of such people as Miss Sims and her sister, Anne Donaldson of Saltcoats in whose circle Albert was then sitting, that had he allowed this manifestation to continue he could have become one of the greatest materialisation mediums of that time.

Laurence remembers his first meeting with Albert in the home circle of Mrs Anne Donaldson when Albert was asked to demonstrate some clairvoyance. Two days before this circle met, Laurence's daughter had witnessed the death by electrocution of a neighbour's child, and he and his wife had prayed for the soul of this child. On the evening of the circle Albert, now in trance, turned to Laurence Goss and the voice of his Guide said, "Mr Goss, the spirit of young Joyce Walker has just awakened in the Spirit world and the guides here tonight wish to thank you and your wife for the prayers you have sent."

Laurence claims that Albert knew nothing of the girl's death and he says this was his first convincing evidence from Spirit. After this he and Albert became great friends, and Albert asked him if he would accompany him to Church services so that Laurence would give the address before Albert demonstrated his mediumship. He also worked with Albert and his healing guide, Dr Wong, and it was Dr Wong who taught Laurence to become a channel for healing. In the early 1950s he assisted Albert at the healing circle in Kilmarnock Church and also accompanied him to a circle in Troon run by a Mrs Bruce. He also mentions that Albert was encouraged to move to Glasgow, give up his work in the Post Office and heal in a sanctuary in Newton Mearns.

Laurence says he will never forget Albert, not only for the brilliant mediumship and healing that he witnessed, but also for the help and evidence given to him and his wife after the death of their daughter Carol at the age of twenty-four. He says that maybe the most important reason for not forgetting Albert is that he was such a good friend.

3
Albert at Thornhill

A businessman who lived near Glasgow and who had retired from business in 1959 after a heart attack, decided one evening to go to a Spiritualist meeting in Troon. He was directed by the Spirit world to provide a room in his property for healing purposes.

He was very impressed by Albert Best and asked him to give up his job in the Post Office and work as his groundsman and full-time healer, and a flat was acquired in Mount Florida, Glasgow and he went to the house regularly to work and to heal.

In 1965 the house caught fire and although the brickwork was burnt on both sides the healing sanctuary remained untouched. The fireman couldn't understand this because there was a very strong wind that day, and while the flames shot up to the door of the sanctuary they didn't penetrate the room. A hut in the grounds was used temporarily, and then a new sanctuary, Thornhill, a quarter of a mile away was opened, and the curtains from the original sanctuary were transferred there. Albert healed in this sanctuary until it was closed in 1982, accompanied by several assistants, and they were always very busy, with Albert being the principal healer directing the others.

Many wonderful healings took place, and Ann Docherty, one of the healers and a very good friend to Albert, sent the following account:

"Thornhill was not a Spiritualist Healing Centre, it was non-denominational. In fact Albert and I were the only Spiritualists within the healing group.

Albert at Kilmarnock, early 1950s

The house itself was in a beautiful setting, surrounded by acres of ground, wonderful trees, birds and flowers, with Highland cattle grazing in one field, and there was a most peaceful atmosphere.

The room dedicated and set aside for healing was large, with three doctor's couches and seating accommodation for about twenty-five people. Healing was available by appointment only, three afternoons and evenings each week, one day being set aside for children.

Albert with medium Evelyn Keeble at Stansted, 1980

The doors were closed before healing started and no one was allowed to enter or leave whilst healing was in progress as Albert was a trance healer.

Dr Wong, Hans and Ally were the Spirit helpers who worked through Albert. I think Dr Wong came through for the more urgent cases, and when he did his presence was a wonderful experience, one strongly felt his love, compassion and peace. When working with Albert it was as if his hand was penetrating the body, but not of course cutting the flesh.

Drawing something from within, he would then plunge his hand into a basin of water to which disinfectant had been added. It was my understanding that this was to dematerialise the substance removed, but I have no proof of this. Hans and Ally, whilst healing, often brought loved ones from the Spirit world who would prove their identity and give a meaningful message, which in itself was the healing some people needed. The love, peace and healing energy experienced in that dedicated sanctuary was truly wonderful. I know without a shadow of doubt all who entered there were blessed and received healing according to their individual needs of body, mind and spirit. I am still of the opinion that the healing we witnessed was personal and private. Hopefully some people who benefited will send their testimonies.

Approximately twenty-four thousand people received treatment at the sanctuary during the twenty-odd years it was open, from Albert and the band of dedicated healers. Albert gave much of his time to healing and many people had good reason to thank God for what they received. I am sure Albert is reaping his rewards now."

4

Make me a Channel of your Peace

Albert visited India on four occasions, staying with old friends and giving a number of sittings to people in need. The friend with whom he stayed, Mrs Hem Singh, visited England every year and of course saw Albert often at the London Spiritual Mission when he was with us. On one occasion I witnessed an extraordinary healing. One Friday morning in July, Albert was giving a sitting to Hem Singh and her husband in our Church library, and I was working in my office in the Church house, when my doorbell rang and Mr Singh, looking decidedly worried, told me I was needed in the library. When I entered, thinking perhaps Albert had been taken ill, I was greeted by the voice of Dr Wong who told me to sit down and listen to him! He informed me that Mrs Singh was entering hospital the following Monday and had been told she would be in there for at least three weeks as she had gall stones and also a stone in the kidney.

This fact I already knew from Hem herself. Dr Wong stated that he wished to perform an operation on the Monday morning and when I told him Albert was going home to Glasgow the following day, Saturday, as he had to take a Sunday Service at his local Church, he said he was quite aware of this. But he insisted I telephone his 'Boss man' and ask him to arrange for Albert to fly up to London early on the Monday morning, and to meet Mrs Singh at the church at noon, when Dr Wong would perform the operation. Hem had to report to the hospital at 4pm that afternoon. He told me that she would have only a small operation and would be in hospital for just four days returning home on the fifth day.

When Albert came out of his deep trance and saw me sitting in with his friends, he asked me in no uncertain terms what I thought I was doing. He was more than a little cross when he heard he had to return South again on the Monday, but finally agreed that Dr Wong's wishes must be met.

When Albert and Hem Singh arrived on Monday morning, Albert asked Nan Mackenzie, who was giving healing at the Church, if she would care to assist, and I was told I was to be the one to hold the basin of water and disinfectant for him. All went well and Dr Wong seemed satisfied with the outcome. Hem reported to the hospital and Albert stayed on with me for a couple of days before returning to Glasgow. Five days later Mrs Singh telephoned me to say she was home, the gallstones had been removed, but the bigger operation did not take place as after a further x-ray they found the stone in the kidney had disappeared. Certainly an experience I shall never forget.

Albert had many wonderful times during his visits to India, and particularly enjoyed visiting a village near Simla in the Himalayas, which he said was an awe-inspiring experience he would never forget.

Morag and James Darroch of Greenock have written the following tribute to our friend Albert and his wonderful gifts:

"It was February 1969 when Albert entered our lives. More importantly, he was introduced to our nine-month-old daughter Janice.

To be blunt, our daughter's life was literally wasting away. She had no control or power in any of her muscles, and in effect couldn't even suck on a bottle. It took about five hours to feed her a small drop of milk. We were told by top doctors and specialists in Glasgow that they could do no more for her and that they were baffled by her illness. Their opinion was that she was probably suffering from Werdning Hoffman's disease, a muscle wasting illness which was very rare indeed, although they didn't or couldn't confirm this! We thought our decision to release our child from hospital and take her home was the best thing to do. On the journey home we noticed that she had become very aware that she had been taken from the hospital environment and was with the two people who loved her, as her features took on a more contented look. We knew immediately that we had made the correct decision, but we also knew deep down, that only a miracle could save her.

So back to February 1969 and Albert Best's appearance. His instructions were that on no account were we to move the baby and he insisted on coming to our home accompanied by three or four dedicated healers. Albert asked me to hold my child, but Morag and I were not sure what, if anything at all, would happen. I remember peaceful music, a dim light and very strong heat going through my body and presumably being transmitted to the baby. In what seemed only a minute or two, but was probably longer, Albert requested that my wife Morag take Janice. 'Please feed her,' said Albert, and to our astonishment and delight Janice began to suck her bottle with great vigour and in no time she had finished it, whilst later that day our child used her muscles to pass her waste food, a previously impossible task.

Albert's wonderful treatment had begun. The three of us were constantly in touch with him as Janice grew older. It was quite obvious that Janice was unwell, but she had great spirit and determination to fight her many problems, and she got to know and love Albert, with complete faith in him. This, we are sure, carried her through year after year, but of course our love and attention played no small part too and we went to great lengths to find a complete cure. However, specialists at the famous Mayo Clinic in Minnesota were also baffled by Janice's illness. All were impressed by her courage. Though never a day passed when she wasn't in pain, her great sense of humour, which was second to none, was not blunted.

Albert Best, year after year, continued to amaze us with his hands on treatment with Janice and she left feeling 'Up for the world ahead' after every visit. One simple incident we recall was when Janice had been suffering pain from toothache all day long, but on meeting Albert the pain was removed within seconds.

Janice had a serious gene defect and never weighed more than four stones, but she received great strength from her visits to Albert. She passed her driving test, and that wasn't easy considering her lack of leg power. She lived life to the full, was a Girls' Brigade Officer and met her 'pop' idol, Paul Young. She was a very popular young lady and worked as an assistant librarian.

Without Albert's constant attention could she have achieved so much in her twenty-three years? Janice died at Christmas in 1991 and when Albert heard the sad news he remarked that she was now 'as free as a bird'. Morag and I continued to visit Albert and without going into details, he told us things about the funeral and repeated comments from Janice of which only we were aware. These were very touching moments.

We were saddened to hear of Albert's death. It was a great privilege to know him, to speak to him, to watch him performing his healing. We will always remember him and be grateful to him for the extended life he gave to our youngest daughter."

Betty and Ian Forbes of Greenock have sent me the following story:

"It was the year 1970 when we first met Albert Best. He was giving healing to our baby daughter, Evelyn, who was twenty-one-months-old. She had a rare blood disease and was not expected to live for more than a few weeks. We believe that it was through the intervention of Albert that we had the pleasure of her company for another nine months, though unfortunately she died in February 1972, and was laid to rest with a little gold cross around her neck. Only with the support of Albert and the Spiritualist Church were my wife and I able to carry on during this very sad period. In December 1972 my wife and I visited the Largs Spiritualist Church where Albert was the guest medium.

During the service he came to my wife and me and gave us the following message. He said that within six (could be days, weeks, or even months) you will receive a cross. This will be a sign that your daughter is on her way. Our interpretation at that time, was that we would receive an apport of a cross and our daughter would have moved to a higher plane.

Nothing happened for five months. In June 1973, which is the sixth month of the year and was also six months from the time of the message, my wife and I attended the Balham Church in London to see Albert at work. After the service we were introduced to a Catholic Priest who had the gift of diagnosis. With the naked eye he could describe your ailments. He looked at my wife and said that she was pregnant, though even the doctor my wife attended was unaware of this at the time.

He also stated that the baby would be a girl. As the Priest was leaving our company he said 'I feel compelled to do this,' and he removed from around his neck a cross (not a crucifix) and handing it to my wife told her to give it to her little girl when she was seven years old.

Everything we were told by Albert and the Priest came true."

One of the most moving and exciting stories of healing given through Albert was that of Lee and Jack McDowell of Lurgan, N. Ireland. They write that no record of Albert's life would be complete without the following details being included:

"That it was a super normal occurrence goes without saying, for there was no known cure at that time for our son. None that we had heard of anyway, and the prospect of critical surgery and a lifetime after of daily medication was appalling. When we were at our lowest point there was Albert, like a lovely, tubby angel, *sans* wings, giving us hope when we had none. We wrote and told John what had happened and we all started to lift our heads again and hope. That was a joyful day for us, we can tell you! An ordinary day perhaps for Albert but not for us. How many more Good News days must there be for countless families all over the countries Albert has travelled, if the truth were known? And it should be and that is why we are telling our tale.

Our son John had been seriously ill for some time. Attending hospital one week in four, where he had undergone tests for Giantism, a condition which affects one person in ten thousand. We were very worried indeed, for his condition was progressively worsening, and it seemed that all the doctors could offer was surgery and a strict regimen of drugs for the rest of his young life.

The events of that Sunday in October will always remain crystal clear in our minds as long as we live. We had left the hospital after visiting our son and had driven through the city to the Malone Avenue Church. There we sat with heavy hearts, for the Specialist's news had not been good – the outlook was bleak indeed. We were desperate, and it seemed that there was no one we could turn to for help, when Albert Best who was demonstrating that morning came to us. 'Mrs McDowell, I have an Ernie Crangle here,' he said (my father's name). 'He is saying to me that he knows the trouble you are having and his message is 'As King Canute had stilled the tide, the tide has been stemmed, worry no more, all will be well'.'

As was said this was in the month of October. November and December passed with John attending hospital, his condition unchanged. January came and after the usual exhaustive tests had been carried out, one of the doctors questioned our son closely. He wanted to know what had happened in the interim period, for the hormonal imbalance which had been causing the trouble all along had suddenly stabilized. It was a complete mystery to the medical team and the doctor in the end admitted to our lad that 'something in the nature of a miracle has happened!' Tests were carried out regularly for some considerable time afterwards, but each time he received a clean bill of health. Now well over twenty years later he enjoys perfect health. The problem has gone forever.

It has been a matter of some personal regret to us, knowing Albert as we did for over a quarter of a century, that so many people seemed unable to see beyond the humanity of the man to the highly perceptive person who guarded his mediumship so carefully; the very private person for whom the urge to help was paramount and money of no importance whatsoever. One could well say the title of his biography could read *The loneliness of the Long Distance Runner*, for he was ever a lonely man, lonely, listening to voices from another dimension and, true to postal tradition, making sure the messages were delivered! There'll never be another like Albert."

5

Albert The Messenger

Two very interesting incidents have been forwarded by Mrs Isobel Bryan of Dunoon, Argyll:

"I first came across Albert Best in the autumn of 1969, one year after losing my six-year-old son with a brain tumour. A friend's mother attended his healing sanctuary at Newton Mearns, and whilst giving her healing he sometimes received communication for her from Spirit. To my astonishment she telephoned me one morning to say that while at the sanctuary the previous evening my son had communicated, giving details which were absolutely correct, and of which neither she nor Albert could have known. After this incident I had several outstanding sittings with Albert when wonderful evidence was given. For several years I attended the healing sanctuary, and the incident I wish to relate happened on one of these occasions.

Just before Christmas 1970 or 1971 – I cannot recall which – I had an appointment at the healing sanctuary on the Friday evening, but had just come out of hospital after having a minor surgical operation, and didn't feel well enough to drive.

Having made enquiries, I was fortunate enough to be telephoned by one of the healers, saying that there was a place for me in their car, and I would be picked up later, and this was a great relief to me. I was the only female in the car, and on the journey the men all talked football etc., so I hardly spoke at all and certainly told no one anything about myself. It was customary for everyone to gather in the large kitchen before making our way into the room which was used for healing, and as we were a little late in arriving, we were ushered hurriedly into the sanctuary. The point I am trying to make is that I told no one of my surgery, and even if I had, this information could not have been passed on to Albert.

The healing session always began with prayer, and background music was played. Albert tuned in and assigned the healers their various patients. I always received healing from one of the other healers, never from Albert, and to my astonishment, after attending to his first patient, Albert suddenly announced, 'I have changed my plans, I will see Mrs Bryan tonight.' I was helped on to the couch, where Albert began to tell me in detail about the operation I had had, repeating almost word for word what the surgeon had told me, including the diagnosis that my problem had been caused by a hormone imbalance. After receiving healing, I returned to my seat.

A little later, I heard Albert say to his assistant 'Tell Mrs Bryan to come back. Her boy wishes to speak to her.'

Albert then proceeded to give me details which my son wished to pass on to me as evidence, but to my intense disappointment none of it made any sense to me.

These incidents were as follows:

1. A Marks and Spencer's plastic carrier bag had burst in the street and the shopping had been scattered over the pavement. Another person had come on the scene and helped to retrieve it. This, he said, happened three months ago.

2. A necklace with a broken clasp was being taken to the jeweller to be repaired.

3. Within the next few days I would receive lily-of-the-valley in some shape or form (this in the middle of winter).

4. Someone had broken their left wrist which was now in plaster.

Albert said that my son was trying to prove to me that the medium was not reading my mind. All these incidents were unknown to me, but I would hear of all of them within the next few days. A few days later, as my cleaning lady and I were sitting chatting over coffee round the kitchen table, she enquired how I had fared on the Friday evening, and was relieved to hear that I had managed to get a lift. 'Did Mr Best tell you anything interesting?' she enquired. I replied that nothing he had told me had made any sense and told her of the incident with the M & S plastic bag. 'That's strange,' she said, 'that's what happened to me, but he couldn't have meant me because that happened back in September.' Albert had in fact said that this had happened three months ago. She confirmed that another lady had helped to pick up her shopping and had produced another carrier bag into which she packed it.

I then told her of the necklace with the broken clasp which was being taken in for repair. With an astonished look on her face she reached into her bag and produced the necklace which she planned to take to the jeweller on her way home.

After we finished our coffee she disappeared to continue her work and I opened several Christmas cards which had been delivered. I could hardly believe my eyes to see that one card depicted a spray of lily-of-the-valley with a sprig of holly!

On Boxing Day, I telephoned my brother who lived in Essex. He told me that his son, who at that time was about twelve-years-old, had had a fall and broken his wrist, adding sarcastically, 'But I thought your spirits would have told you that.'

There was a stunned silence at the other end of the telephone when I replied, 'Well, if it's his left wrist then they did.' Needless to say, it was his left wrist!

The second incident happened several years later on one of my many visits to Stansted Hall, Albert Best being the resident medium that week. My brother Jack lived in Essex not far from Stansted Mountfitchet, and he usually came over for a visit while I was there. On this particular occasion I toyed with the idea of trying to persuade him to come to Albert's demonstration in the Sanctuary. I sent out a thought to our father, who at that time had been in Spirit for about twenty-five years, asking him to communicate with Jack if I was successful in persuading him to come. I also asked him to speak of something that happened when he was in the RAF that I knew absolutely nothing about, so that there could be no suspicion of collusion between me and the medium.

He and his wife were a little late arriving that evening, due to problems with the car, but I did manage to persuade my brother to go to the demonstration, although he only agreed to please me. During the service Albert pointed to me, saying that my father and my son were there, but they didn't want to speak to me, but with the gentleman sitting beside me. He told my brother that he almost hadn't made it that evening due to problems with his car, only arriving 'On a wing and a prayer'. He said that he had been at a garage looking at cars for sale, and quoted to him the prices painted on the windscreen of each car he looked at. Then he said 'That expression I used 'On a wing and a prayer' – that's an RAF expression, and you were in the RAF and whilst with them you flew aeroplanes.' This was true as my brother had been a cadet pilot and had flown solo. 'Something went wrong and you panicked. You didn't know it at the time, but you received help to bring the plane down safely. You went from blind panic to icy calm and knew exactly what you must do.'

He then described how, as my brother was bringing the plane in to land, he flew between a tree on one side and a water tank on the other, to land safely. As I listened to this in amazement I was thinking, 'This is rubbish. I've never heard this,' completely forgetting that I had made the request to Spirit to make it something I knew nothing about. As we left the Sanctuary I asked my brother if what Albert had told him had been true, and he nodded in agreement, being almost speechless with shock. While my brother was in the RAF he often spent 48-hour leaves

Albert with Nan MacKenzie 1982

with an aunt who lived in London, and when I related this story to her it turned out that he had told her of this incident while staying with her all those years ago, and had made her promise never to tell anyone."

Ann Docherty, who has already given details of the wonderful healing which took place at Thornhill, tells of the first piece of evidence she received from Spirit in her early days of searching which came through Albert at a public meeting in Berkeley Street Church. Ann still regularly attended the Church of Scotland, and this was the first meeting of Albert's to which she had gone. Albert was looking for someone who could accept a young man by the name of Ronald who was in spirit. Ann says she did not respond but someone else did and Albert would not accept this person. He pointed to Ann and said "You can take Ronald."

Ann said she nearly passed out, her heart was pounding and she could only nod her head in the affirmative. Albert continued, "I am being told you are very concerned about someone who is very close to you, and you have been praying for healing for that person." Again she could only nod her head. Albert said "Well, your prayers are heard and are being answered. Jesus heals today as he did in the days of old, but always remember, there is a time for healing. This comes from Ronald, it's the first time he has come through to you since he passed," and he continued by giving her the day, month and year.

Ann says that thirteen years earlier she had given birth to a much wanted baby boy after years of waiting. Tragically he lived for one day only. Ronald was the name they had chosen for him, and no one in the world except her husband, herself and the doctor who attended the birth knew this.

Since the experience was too painful to dwell upon, Ann did her best to put it all behind her, fully believing her baby had returned to Jesus and having no idea that a little child could grow up in a Spirit world. She could not even remember the date of the infant's passing, but on checking at home she realised that Albert was absolutely correct in every detail. Ann sums up this touching story with the words:

"What a wonderful experience that was for me. Here was my son, whom I had never even held in my arms, coming back to comfort me and to open the doors into a new world for me. I thank God for Albert, he certainly was used to lead me into pastures new, to open my mind to the Spirit World."

Pietro Alexander Nardini, 1962 - 1982

Sandra Nardini, mother of Pietro writes:

"I first met Albert Best in 1984, two years after my son Pietro was killed in a road accident.

A friend who was a member of the Berkeley Street Spiritualist Church had a sitting booked with Albert, and persuaded my husband to take her place. Albert had no idea who was coming into the room, if he had read his appointments earlier he would have seen '2 pm Catherine', but instead received a tall, rather embarrassed man who was obviously at a loss for words. Albert went straight to the facts. The facts of the accident, the place where it happened and the agony it caused the family. Albert had a direct line to our son.

I was sitting outside in the hall, and afterwards when my husband came out he looked a totally different man. He was born and raised a Roman Catholic, and he had enough faith to know that there is an afterlife, but he knew that I had to have proof. The reason I did not go in for the sitting is that I had already seen Albert and had been attending his meetings, and I know it was terrible to be suspicious but I thought he might have heard something about what had happened and so I sent in my husband who was unknown to Albert.

The strange things that happened after this meeting were that Pietro usually 'came' to Albert when he was on his own in his flat, and Albert used to telephone and say 'Sandra, I've got your boy here, he tells me you have changed the colour of your hair!' Another time he telephoned to say 'Your boy tells me you have bought a piano,' which I had two days before, and then one Sunday, and this is amazing proof,

Albert called to say 'Your boy is asking if you all enjoyed your rhubarb pie.' Pietro knew we never ate rhubarb but that particular morning my husband was pottering about in the garden and came in with a handful of rhubarb and said 'I think I'll make a rhubarb pie!' Words cannot express what Albert contributed to our family. The only thing he ever accepted was a whisky – the only thing he ever wanted was friendship. He was an amazing man, without him or my being guided to him, I think I would have lost more than my son, I think I may have lost my sanity."

Help at Hand

In 1987 I received a telephone call from a friend telling me of a great tragedy which had taken place in Scotland to a family well known to her and asking if I could suggest anyone who could help. My immediate reaction was they should see Albert Best, and as he was then in South Africa, I suggested they should write to him at his home in Glasgow, the letter to await his return. A simple letter asking to see him, but giving no details.

Irene and Jim Stewart of Ballantrae write as follows:

"We are writing to tell you how Albert helped us and later became a good friend.

Our daughters were killed in a car accident on Christmas Eve in 1986. Through a friend we wrote to Albert.

He was at the time in South Africa, but when he came home he wrote to us with his telephone number to get in touch, which we did. It was as if we were listening to the girls telling us they were all right. Lots of everyday things which to other people meant nothing, but to us were so very important. We think the most amazing thing of all was that on seeing their photographs he could tell us which one was which, and he knew their names which we had never mentioned to him. We could go on and on giving you more and more proof. We didn't need any more.

As Albert always said 'They are only a room away.' Some day we will be with them. Perhaps we were fortunate in that Catrina and Irene have each other, just as we have each other, some people are left completely on their own."

Two very courageous people.

"Thank You, Albert" from the Countess of Inchcape.

"I first started seeing Albert Best many years ago when I was trying to help Scottish friends who had lost both children in a tragic car accident. It was chance (or was it?) that Albert lived in nearby Glasgow, although I had received his name from Rosalind Cattanach in London. I was so impressed with the way he helped them that I decided to have a sitting myself.

I had many subsequent yearly sittings and he never failed to give me precious communications from family and friends.

My mother had died shortly before my first sitting with Albert, and on the second or third sitting when she came through remarked that she had been with me and my middle child Ailsa at our local village church the previous Sunday.

She proceeded to give me two hymns that we had indeed sung during that service. I was fairly certain they were the very hymns and this was verified by Ailsa. There are 799 hymns in the 'Ancient and Modern'!!

On another occasion, dear Nan MacKenzie came through and remarked that she had been with me when I was writing my poetry of late. This astounded me as no one knew I was writing poetry during a rather difficult period of my life. She said that she hoped I would one day write it from joy rather than stress!

What a special man Albert was, and how much solace and comfort he brought to so many people. For me, it was as much the familiar manner of speaking of those he brought through as the factual demonstrations of particular instances of life that gave me proof. The subtlety of his mediumship was extraordinary. Those of us who benefited from his talent and compassion were indeed fortunate." Georgina Inchcape.

Alex Irons of Bournemouth writes the following true story concerning the superb mediumship which he and his late wife Ann experienced back in the 1970s. He says that the passage of time has not lessened in any way the impact, or detracted from the profound impression this made upon both of them:

"My late wife Ann and I spent the Christmas and New Year holiday in 1971 visiting with her eldest brother Price and his wife Mabel at their home in El Monte, California, and during our stay with them we also visited the homes of members of Mabel's immediate family who were living in the vicinity.

One of Mabel's brothers, Clement (Clem) and his wife Helen had their daughter and son-in-law staying with them over the festive season, and we were introduced to them when we were invited there for lunch. About a year later we received a letter from Price to tell us that Clem and Helen's daughter and her husband had been involved in an horrific car accident on a local freeway. The daughter, though badly injured, made a good recovery, but her husband after ten days in a deep coma, had died from the results of the multiple injuries which he had sustained.

A few months later Ann and I attended a Sunday evening service at Balham Spiritualist Church where Albert was the visiting medium, and the following is a true account of what transpired. Pointing directly at me Albert said "Battersea, I want Battersea with you, but I have to give someone else a message first. I will return to you later." As both my parents and myself had been born and bred in Battersea I could accept what Albert had said regarding my association with that area. Returning to me a few minutes later he said 'I don't want Battersea with you now, that was only the link. I want America. I want the Pacific Coast of America. I want California. I have a young man here who says that you once met when you were out there. He died as a result of an accident in which he was involved on a freeway. He speaks of the wheels spinning round and of the terrible long

Albert as the "Sheik of Araby"
Stansted Concert 1982

period of blackness. He speaks of Clement and Helen and wishes them to know that he is now OK.'

Price and Mabel were very staunch and strict Methodists, pillars of their local Church, and looked upon our beliefs as 'the works of the devil'. They had covertly made it quite obvious that they privately thought Ann and I must be 'ten cents short of a dollar'! Returning home in the car from the service at Balham we were pondering on how we could best handle this situation, and after a prolonged discussion and lengthy debate at home, we came to the conclusion that we should honour the young man's expressed wishes in a straightforward and matter-of-fact way. I wrote to Price and Mabel and gave them an honest account of what had happened, but the result was a stony silence. We did not receive a reply to our letter for an abnormally long time, and when it did arrive the part dealing with this remarkable matter was completely ignored.

Whilst it is a great truism that 'There are none so blind as those who do not wish to see' and 'None so deaf as those who do not wish to hear' both Price and Mabel have since made their transitions and will no doubt have come to realise that Ann and I were not so 'far off the beam' as they previously thought, and as Ann has also since passed, she will have been able to put the record straight for them. We did our best at the time to honour the request that had been made to us through Albert's remarkable, excellent and evidential mediumship – whether or not the details were passed to Clem and Helen we shall never know."

Mr Albert Allan of Southborough sent me details of what was extraordinary conclusive proof of true communication:

"In July 1979 I was fortunate to have a private sitting with Albert Best at Pembridge Place Church. He reunited me with my younger sister who died in a road accident fifty-eight years earlier aged seven. He specified her injuries, stated she sent her love to her three brothers and sister, mentioned the four roses on her coffin from her four siblings; my rank in the Army; family members who had passed on and had been welcomed by her, and that she would be at a family wedding later in 1979. Albert Best described her as she was in 1921 and that she was so excited at communicating she was dancing around and wouldn't keep still.

During the sitting I asked Albert for her name and he told me to be patient and he would ask her. Some minutes later she told him her name was Jessie Allan. Absolutely correct. To my mind a wonderful sitting and a stirring experience for me."

The following details sent to me show how our Spirit friends can help us when the need arises if we trust sufficiently:

"Many years ago the firm I had worked with for seventeen years closed down and the employees were given redundancy. I was given the option to work for another branch in the same capacity. At the time I thought this was the best option. However, I found that it was not what I had been used to and was very unhappy in this situation. I continued to work there although I dreaded going in. My husband did not know how I felt for I knew if he did he would have made me leave, and I thought it was for the good of the family that I stuck it out.

One day I read in the paper about a meeting in the Spiritualist Church that was being taken by a Mr Albert Best, whom I had previously seen on television. I felt I wanted to go to this meeting and my husband encouraged me. I didn't know quite what to expect, the Church was packed but I managed to find a seat right at the back. When Mr Best started his demonstration the first thing he said was could anyone take an Alex McLean? I couldn't have answered but someone in the centre of the hall did. However, Albert Best said that was not right, the message was for a lady right at the back, and he pointed to me. He said that it was a private message and he would see me after the service. When the meeting finished the steward asked me to go into the medium's room. When Mr Best came in he said that my boss Alex McLean (who had died about a year previously) was very concerned about me. The message went on to say he thought he had taught me better than that. He said I was to go to the head of the firm and tell him that my being in my present position was their idea and it hadn't worked out, so I wished to be made redundant and take early retirement as if I was still working for the original firm. This seemed impossible as the firm had closed down seven months previously. It was almost as if Alex McLean himself was speaking. He mentioned a tall red-haired gentleman who was also with him and wished to be remembered to me. This was one of the travellers who had been killed in an accident some years ago.

When I spoke to the personnel officer and said I was leaving and wished to be considered for redundancy from my original firm, he told me I didn't have a hope as too much time had passed since the closure. I then got in touch with the directors of the firm and put my request to them. To my delight, after some discussion they agreed and I was given my redundancy and also my early retirement.

I am very grateful to Mr Best for conveying the message and to my boss for caring enough to make it possible for me to receive his instructions and thereby act on them to my advantage."

Mr Dennis Sadler of Mildenhall writes:

"I regard Albert Best as one of the most evidential mediums I have witnessed in my thirty years in Spiritualism. I first experienced his mediumship in the late sixties in an evening service at Harley Church, Ipswich, which was run by Edna Wardle and Jack Robinson. In the demonstration of clairvoyance Albert went to a friend and police colleague of mine who was sitting some distance from me in the crowded meeting, and brought him evidence of his son who had recently passed with muscular dystrophy. Albert then came to me and told me that the son of the last recipient was also known to me, which was correct. There was no way Albert could have known I had any connection with this man. For the next few years Albert made an annual visit to Harley Church and I made every effort to attend the services he took. For some reason he seemed to come to us with a message on most occasions.

Then there was a break of many years in my contact with Albert. Meantime both Jack Robinson and Edna Wardle passed to Spirit round about 1987 and 1989, and my police colleague passed in May 1991.

I next experienced Albert's mediumship when I attended an 'Albert Best Week' at Stansted Hall in November 1991. My wife and I arrived on the Saturday, but we did not speak to Albert until he came to me during the Sunday service demonstration of clairvoyance. It had been about twenty years since I had previously seen him and I do not think he had placed me, although one cannot be sure. My wife switched on the tape recorder and later transcribed the recording."

The following is a precis of what was received.

Albert said 'There's a policeman walking up and down. Wonder who he's after. Would you know a policeman who has just passed away? 'Cos he says you were in the force together. He says Stow ... something Stow.' The recipient replied that Stowmarket was a town he was familiar with. Albert continued 'This policeman says he was your colleague. Do you understand?' This was confirmed. 'He's been brought by a lady and she shows me peas.' Mr and Mrs Sadler remembered Miss Wardle had lived on peas in her last few months. 'She's brought this policeman through and she's laughing about the peas. She says she's still working and tells you not to give up. Do you understand what she means? Are you retiring or retired?' Dennis stated he had retired from one job and was now doing another. Albert enquired if he wore a stripe and Dennis confirmed that he did at one time and his colleague was also a sergeant. Albert continued by saying that this lady hadn't forgotten Dennis and that she no longer needed her peas! Dennis told Albert he also knew this lady well himself and that she was Edna Wardle. Albert seemed surprised and continued 'She says you have been sending out thoughts to her and she is laughing about this, telling you it must have been about twenty-five years, but she's happy to meet you here tonight and Jack is here too. It's the first time she's come to let you know.' Dennis Sadler confirmed this.

Albert as The Oldest Swinger in town,
Stansted Concert 1984

Dennis Sadler concludes "Although I received other evidence from Albert at the services I attended and at a private sitting I had at Stansted Hall, I think the details I have related of the two incidents which occurred over twenty years are remarkable. I do not think they can be accounted for by thought-reading. The only way Albert could have known the details given was that he spoke with knowledge received by him from inhabitants of the Spirit world."

A tribute from Alan Ross of Alan Ross Publishing, Lantana, Florida:

"It was 1984 and I had just been introduced to Spiritualism a year earlier when I came to England. Upon my arrival in London I found my way to a small hotel in Bayswater. The next day I purchased *Psychic News* and in the church listings I saw that the closest church to where I was staying was The London Spiritual Mission, so that Sunday I went to my first Spiritualist church service. It was a charming little church so beautifully decorated with flowers, and the picture of Jesus on the wall basking in God's light instead of bleeding on the cross was so uplifting to me. I remember in the service there were hymns and an address by an Irish/Scottish gentleman, Albert Best.

I had to strain to follow what he was saying because I was not used to such a brogue. Then came time for messages from the dear departed. Mr Best was also the demonstrating medium. He called on a woman in about the fourth row and told her that he had her brother and proceeded to describe his death. 'I was murdered and my body stuffed into the trunk of a car and the whole thing sunk in a marshy bog.' The sister, at the top of her lungs gave out a scream that sent a chill down my spine. She said 'I knew it. I knew it, he was in the rackets.' She then burst into tears. The atmosphere in the little church was so thick you could nearly cut it with a knife.

Mr Best then came to a young man sitting near me. He told

him that his father was there and wanted him to know that it was very difficult for him to express his feelings when he was alive and that he now wanted his son to know that he loved him very much and regretted not being able to tell him. The young man acknowledged that this was true about their relationship, and thought it was something his father would say ...

The last person that I can remember was a man in the back sitting next to the aisle. During the second war he was in a German prison camp. Mr Best had linked with his chum who didn't make it back home. He proceeded to tell details of their captivity and his subsequent death. The former soldier kept nodding his head to everything Albert Best described. I found this quite amazing.

I wasn't called on, but I didn't need to be in order to be convinced that Mr Best had a talent to hear Spirits that I had not witnessed before, and for that matter didn't even know was possible. Later I learned that Albert Best had assisted Scotland Yard in finding missing persons. This was more than enough for me to realise that I had been fortunate indeed to have had such a memorable experience."

6
The Messenger Abroad

Mike Tannett from Betty's Bay, South Africa writes:

How searching for survival led us to Albert Best.

"We lost Mickey our twenty-one-year-old son at sea on 15th April 1988 whilst he was diving for crayfish off Chapman's Peak near Hoult Bay, Cape Town. It was a cold day with a blustering south-easter pushing a swell on to the rocks. His body was recovered six weeks later at Cape Point, some 15 km away.

This was by far the most painful and difficult hurdle in the lives of his parents and two surviving children, for parents who care cannot stop loving or wanting to look after their missing child. 'Is there survival after death and if so is our child in good hands?' we asked the Church Minister after the funeral. 'Oh yes,' he exclaimed. 'Well, please tell us what happens?' we answered. 'Well, there is definitely survival,' we were told but that's where the Church stops. Parents are in such need of comfort, but none is forthcoming. So the search began – through various religions and on into Spiritualism.

Not knowing where to start we discovered some Mediums with various abilities. We read many books including *A Venture in Immortality*. Both my wife Lynda and I were very impressed with the evidence given in this book by the Rev. David Kennedy from a medium called Albert Best, and although we would like to have met him we realised the chance of this was remote.

Only a few months later in February 1989 Albert came to Cape Town for a holiday, and we were one of the few privileged couples to sit with him: He was staying with his friends in Diep

River, a part of Cape Town we had never visited.

Albert did not even look in our direction, just beckoned us to follow. Before I could sit down he said 'There is a young man in the room with us who says his name is Michael, and he tells me your name is Michael so to differentiate he is called Mickey. He is saying your surname Tannett, and his middle name is Lawrence.' As we sat down he said 'He travelled in the car with you from Gordon's Bay. Your son tells me he saw you working on the roof of your house yesterday and that you completed the job.' All this was perfectly correct. This was the greatest treasure for us, it was as if Albert was on a direct telephone to Heaven, for he went on to give the names of my parents and Lynda's parents. He even told me Mickey had met my sister Suzzy who had died when hit by a car in Switzerland in 1948 at the age of three and a half. He turned to Lynda and said 'Your son says there is something in your bag that belonged to him, please empty it on the floor.' Lynda turned her bag upside down and forty items lay on the floor. 'That belongs to him,' said Albert, pointing at a booklet. He was right again!

Two dear friends of ours L. and R. who came to tell us Mickey was missing at sea that terrible night eight years ago were expecting the birth of their first baby in June of 1988, two months after Mickey's accident. This was no ordinary birth as it took L. and R. many visits to Cape Town, 90km away, to visit a specialist at Groote Schuur Hospital month after month for two years before she finally became pregnant.

A week before her baby was due L. had her first dream (or was it something more?). In this dream she saw Mickey with his arm outstretched towards her and she knew without any doubt that Mickey had come to take her baby from her so she tried to run away but every time she looked back there was Mickey with his arms outstretched. A week later L. knew her baby was on the way so they rushed through Cape Town to the hospital. That night her baby was stillborn.

A devastated L. had her second dream that same night. Again she saw Mickey, but this time the baby was in his arms. Two and a half years later Albert gave a public demonstration of clairvoyance at Sea Point. Lynda managed to get seats so we took L. with us. The tickets were sold out, 150 people were packed into this small area. Albert had to walk about giving messages to people. After about twenty minutes he walked back to the stage and pointed straight at L. and said 'I have your baby boy tonight – it lived yet it never lived.' He turned to Lynda sitting separately, and then to me sitting still further away and said 'Your son.' He embraced us from the stage and said again 'Your son has brought this baby here tonight, I only wish you could see him as I do.'

Ten days prior to this meeting, a young man, a friend from work, had tragically shot his wife and himself after the breakdown of a very unhappy marriage. The day after the incident another friend and I had prayed on our lunchtime for him. Albert turned to me again that night and said 'There is a young man here who has come through for the first time. His name is N. – he is coloured, no he is Indian and your son has helped him through tonight.'

We came to know and befriend Albert after that public meeting and wrote to him up until the month before he passed.

He stayed with us for two weekends at Betty's Bay on different trips to South Africa. Whilst sitting at breakfast one Sunday morning he started reeling off names of my parents and friends who had passed, then he mentioned the name L. I had not seen or heard of L. for thirty years since I was at school. We both played cricket for the same club. As a senior he used to coach me and took special interest in my progress.

Geography was the subject he taught, and the only one I achieved in. Yet here was Albert telling me L. had died. It took two days of telephoning before I discovered that Albert was again right. This evidence could not have come from me, it must have come from another source."

The following is a cutting from a Newsletter published in New Zealand, from Eve Higgins, a Minister of the Golden Light Church, Auckland, New Zealand:

"I was very sad to hear the news of the passing of Albert Best for he was the finest clairvoyant I'd ever heard. I first met Albert about fourteen years ago when he came to New Zealand to tour, and I was delighted to see and hear this wee Irishman giving such proof of survival, names and addresses, even telephone numbers, but when he strutted across the stage and began to sing *The Man Who Broke the Bank at Monte Carlo* I cracked up laughing with everyone else.

It was his Spirit contact who asked Albert to sing, he had been a variety artist and was contacting two ladies in the audience who worked on the stage with him, and he named the stage productions!! His evidence was very impressive. We met again at Stansted Hall, the Spiritualist College in Essex in 1989, recalling together our last meeting at Ron Gibbs House for morning tea, where he spoke of Glasgow where he lived, and of my hometown Dundee where he had worked. We had a few laughs with his Irish sense of humour and I was given an impromptu sitting which needless to say was outstanding.

At the Sunday Service at Stansted I received another message via Albert from three mediums, one being the co-founder of my Church of the Golden Light, with excellent evidence of a conversation we had before she passed. The other mediums were Rosie Bates and Edna Croggin. Edna was on form, discussing her wonderful funeral and the Maori choir. I felt very privileged to be given such evidence of survival from three fellow workers in Spirit. Albert was a true servant of the Spirit World, and to many, a great comforter in their grief. Well done thou true and faithful servant."

The following account contains details from Joan and Ken King of Melbourne who hosted Albert when he visited Australia.

Ken King writes:

"My wife Joan and I visited the UK in 1977. Joan knew of Albert Best by reputation but had never met him. After arriving in Glasgow on the Saturday, Joan learned that Albert was to demonstrate at the Dundee Church of the Spirit the next day. We travelled to Dundee and were in the Church when Albert commenced his demonstration. After some time, he came to Joan and asked whether the name Abbotsford meant anything to her. When Joan said it was a suburb in Melbourne, Albert Best continued with a message from a Henry Montgomery who had lived at 77a Park Street, Abbotsford and who knew Ken's parents through Church. I had no knowledge of Henry Montgomery, but when I returned to Melbourne that July I tried to find the house at 77a Park Street. However, the houses at 75/77 and 79/81 had been demolished and two new houses were in the process of construction.

A search of the records at the public library revealed that a semi-detached dwelling was built between numbers 75 and 77 Park Street and was designated 75a and 77a. The records also showed that a Hy. A. Montgomery resided at 77a during the years 1952-1954. However by July 1977 my parents and close relatives had passed so no further investigation was possible. But it was a fact that both of my parents had lived their early years in the vicinity and had been married at a Church close to Park Street, Abbotsford."

Joan King writes:

"At a large public meeting in Melbourne on March 23rd 1984, Albert Best said he had a message for my mother from her son. Then he commenced singing *Oh My Darling Clementine*. He said "Of course his name was not Clementine but Clement – known as Clem." My mother had received proof from that wonderful medium Nan Mackenzie, but Albert was the first to bring forth this name in thirty years.

My mother passed away in 1988 and my sister Kath and I

travelled to the UK the following year. We attended a large public meeting in Brighton during the Edward Street Church's 'Festival of Spiritualism' and Albert Best was the medium on this particular occasion. When he came to me he said 'I make no apology for knowing you, but I have your mother here. She talks about you sending your coffee back – it wasn't nice! And also says 'Fancy them serving the coffee in a teapot!'" This was quite true and happened only the day before when my sister and I had been motoring to Brighton and had stopped for refreshments. Finally, Albert said that she thanked me for the Blue Grass. Not a soul knew that the previous Christmas I had purchased my mother's favourite perfume Blue Grass, in the hope that she would know and be able to take its counterpart with her. I shall never forget this evidence as long as I live."

From Rosamunde Watson at a public meeting held at the Camberwell City Hall, Melbourne, on March 23rd 1984 with Albert Best demonstrating:

"My experience with Albert Best was truly sensational for all the world to hear, namely a very large Camberwell auditorium. The audience was made up of Spiritualists, their friends and seekers. Many of us knew one another and of the incident which I am relating. I took a friend with me who was grieving for his father and who hoped that he would have some message, but no, it was for me. Albert gave several messages to members of the audience, and then he said 'I have a cockatoo, but it isn't a bird. I have Jeff, Old Jeff, he says.'

Old boy was one of my sayings left over from England and I knew then it was Jeff Mauger. He passed in that awful March fire and afterwards I saw Jeff with his face burned and beard pulled, and I got a flash of pain whenever I saw his face, which was often.

I could not get it out of my mind. Through Albert, Jeff said, 'I passed quickly and am so glad to be here, and have no wish to be back again.' Those flashes of Jeff's face still come back but I no longer feel the pain – love for Jeff and Albert and much thanks to the Upstairs Management!"

Note: Jeff Mauger was a close friend of Rosamunde. He lived on his country property at Cockatoo near Melbourne. He was burned to death in an horrific bush fire which destroyed his property some years before Albert Best visited Melbourne.

"A Loving Old Gem"

Mrs Ferosa Aslam Khan from New Delhi writes of Albert as "A loving old Gem with a heart of gold and compassion of a child, that is what Albert was all about."

Introduced to Albert by her older son Afzal, Mrs Khan states she immediately took to Albert with a feeling she had known him all her life. Seventy-eight years of Albert and nineteen years of Afzal seemed to hit it off as if they were childhood buddies. Later Albert told me that he spoke to Afzal as he had never spoken to anyone before. Albert had somehow opened his heart to Afzal, telling him all about his sad childhood and misfortunes of life concerning his wife and children, that he lost during the war. Speaking to Afzal made him feel good and by the end both of them were crying. When Albert declared that Afzal was an old soul with a young body, she did not fully understand his meaning, never previously having been in contact with mediums or Spiritualists. Later of course, it became very clear to her. Before Afzal was killed his mother's life seemed perfect, fulfilment was its name, but when the storm broke her life was shattered, her son was snatched away from her by the games played by destiny. He was no more, but she was still living, wondering how she would carry on with this deep grief within her, but realising that her husband and two other children needed her. Realising one has to carry on – life and death having its own calculations, we are meant to live and die for certain reasons.

Feeling intense numbness, part of her seemed to have died

with her son, leaving her much stronger, giving her power of bearance. She states she now feels stronger than the strongest of human beings – a strange kind of power which death cannot shake any more, being a reality which must be accepted gracefully.

Her friend Mrs Natwar Singh was about to host Albert in Delhi, and arranged for her and her husband to have their first sitting with him since Afzal's departure from this life. Transport problems made them late and they were told by Mrs Singh that Albert was very restless as Afzal was already there.

Anxious to make contact with him Mr and Mrs Khan sat listening to Albert conveying their son's message of his love for them both, and saying they should not worry about him as he was very well looked after by Fatima, whom Albert described, saying that she too had accompanied Afzal to the sitting.

Afzal's description of the lady was exactly like Aslam's aunt, his father's sister who was married to the Nawab of Radhanpur. a state in Gurjat (a province of India). She was a very pious lady but neither Mr nor Mrs Khan knew her name as she was never mentioned by name in the family. They all called her Ammatan, which is an endearment for mother. They were both confused about the name which was later confirmed as correct. Albert also described Aslam's great grandfather Sardar Ayub Khan who too had accompanied Afzal. It was difficult to comprehend this elderly Irishman's knowledge of their family, and from then onwards Albert came as a ray of light and hope to the entire family. That their son Afzal could contact them gave great solace.

Their younger son Asad also had a sitting with Albert during which amazing things took place. To begin with Afzal asked Albert to give his love to Assadi (or Asdi as Albert pronounced it), which Albert couldn't understand but conveyed. Afzal always called Asad Assadi, when he felt a lot of affection for him. Then he told Asad not to keep any kind of hatred inside him for those who killed him, as they would be seriously dealt with after their death, and also that Afzal was saying that he was taken by surprise, he did not see the weapon with which he was shot as it was hidden under a sheet the killer was wearing, and this was what actually happened.

There were lighter moments when their respective girlfriends were mentioned by Afzal through Albert. Asad wanted Afzal to prove his presence. Suddenly the latch of a cupboard kept in Albert's room was released which left the cupboard doors wide open. Albert got up, grumbling that Afzal was again playing games with him, his pyjamas had shifted from his wardrobe to under his pillows. He picked them up and put them back in their place and closed the cupboard.

Earlier during Mr and Mrs Khan's sitting Albert also conveyed to them that there was another young man who had accompanied Afzal, and he described him, telling them that his name was Dinesh. Now Dinesh was Mr Khan's bodyguard who had also died the same day as Afzal. He was accompanying Mr and Mrs Khan to Roorkee to see Afzal, not knowing what had happened. They met with an accident in which Dinesh was killed and Mr and Mrs Khan injured. Albert said that Dinesh was saying he was happy and wanted to send his love to his wife and children, telling them not to worry about him. This was yet another amazing factor, they did not know Albert, and yet he knew every detail of the catastrophe that took place in their lives.

Mr Khan's elder brother Mohd. Akbar Khan was very fond of Afzal. He is a person who loses himself in his thoughts so while driving Afzal always reminded his uncle to change the second gear, and this had become a regular feature with 'Akbar Daddy', the name by which Afzal addressed him.

During a sitting with Albert, Akbar asked Afzal to say something which happened between them, and Afzal conveyed through Albert an instance that only Akbar Agha experienced. He reminded him of the time when driving home from a friend's house Afzal told him the area where he was driving and how without Akbar being aware of it the gear was changed to third, which Akbar put down to his lost attitude. He thought maybe he had changed the gear and had immediately thought of Afzal telling him 'Akbar Daddy, there is a strain on the car if you don't change the gears.' Albert related this whole incident not understanding what it was all about. Albert also said that the gear was changed by Afzal.

Some time before Afzal died, his father Aslam had a sitting with Albert, as of course Afzal had introduced his father to Albert. During that sitting Albert gave Aslam's father's name, he always had difficulty pronouncing Indian and Muslim names, but he managed. He described him, his prominent limp and said 'your father remembers your wound on the knee.' Aslam had got badly hurt above his knee when he was a teenager playing soccer. Also, 'Do you remember my black mark above the ankle?' Aslam's father suffered from eczema that left a mark above the ankle. He also asked Aslam if he remembered his crooked little finger which was most conspicuously crooked. He told Albert to tell his older son, Akbar, not to keep cutting the big mole near his nose while shaving himself, because it would harm him in the long run! Aslam was really taken aback to see this Scots/Irish medium giving all these fine details of his family who lived in Dehra Dun.

Following Afzal's death and during the first sitting they had with Albert, he also mentioned Afzal asking him why those thousands of people were trying to touch him and carry him on their shoulders. According to Albert, when a soul leaves the body, he is in a confused state of mind, he sees himself and then sees his body lying away from him and cannot understand why people are crying, because he does not realise that he does not exist any more for this world and that a common human eye cannot see his soul. Afzal told Albert he could see his friend Jagat when he was carrying him after what had happened to him. They told Albert that this was the funeral where all his friends, and thousands of people had walked carrying him, giving shoulder through his last journey.

After they had a few sittings with Albert they felt and realised that their son was just a thought away, which was of great support to their broken hearts. They invited Albert to Dehra Dun and brought him to Afzal's home, as he called it. He met the family and was very much at ease and comfortable. He would converse with Mr Khan's mother, aged eighty, who did not know English, just a word here and there, and of course Albert had no clue about Hindi or Persian (the mother's language), but the two of them would comfortably spend mornings together. Albert had a soothing effect on some and very disturbing on others, as we shall see later.

Every time Mrs Khan would enter Albert's room she would find him in conversation either in French or English. Once she walked in and saw Albert in the bathroom crying and saying "I love you too, I love you too." She heard this because Albert never closed the door properly! When he came out he said that Afzal kept saying "I love you, Mr Best!!" Albert was himself amazed at the love he had for Afzal. That same evening, visiting his grave, it had a strange effect on Albert, he sobbed like a baby. He gave sittings to every member of the house, telling them things that only Afzal could say, which kept the family thinking.

One day Mr Khan had a visitor, a Deputy Inspector General, whose wife and daughter had recently died in a car accident but this man was soon up to games! They knew his background but Albert knew nothing. By now with experience, the Khans knew Albert's every move. Mrs Khan saw Albert looking behind the Inspector and trying to say something under his breath, trying to chase away who was bothering him. Seeing this she went and sat next to Albert and asked him what had happened. He then asked her if the man had lost two women in his family, one younger and one older, and described them. The older he said had a big round vermillion spot on her forehead (which is worn by Hindu married women) and a young girl of nineteen/twenty years of age.

Albert said they were wanting to make contact with the Detective Inspector, although his wife did not look happy about something. Sometimes Albert had a twinkle in his eye when he found something amusing. She knew exactly what was happening in her husband's life and the twinkle in Albert's eye told Mrs Khan that he knew it too. Albert asked the Inspector if he would like to have a sitting with him. He looked uncomfortable but agreed to this. What happened inside there the Khans could not know, but the Detective Inspector looked very flustered when he came out, hurriedly wished them goodbye and left the house. He did not visit them again for a very long time.

Albert's health did not allow him to visit India again. He went out shopping and bought all his friends little gifts. His love was transparent and he was greatly loved by all. His visit, his knowledge, his presence helped the Khan family tremendously, and they did not want him to go, but of course he had to leave and promised to keep in touch.

His last message through Mrs Natwar Singh was that Afzal asked them to look for a copper coin with a hole in it in his coin collection. When they went to Dehra Dun Mrs Khan looked for it in the box which held his collection of coins, but was disappointed not to find it there. The next day when she was cleaning her daughter's room she found a little box which belonged to her younger son Asad; Afzal in his generous moods would give a few coins to Asad. On opening it there was the copper coin with the hole in it staring at her. It gave her a strange feeling of closeness towards her son and as he had conveyed to Albert "Tell my mother to keep this coin with her always." She will now have it with her as long as she lives.

Albert opened the windows of the unknown world for the Khan family who now understand that all is not lost and they will all meet some day. Mrs Khan says they pray for his soul to rest in peace each and every day knowing that all have to make this ultimate journey.

7
The Poltergeist

Professor Archie Roy, who has written the Foreword to this short tribute to Albert, relates in his very interesting book *A Sense of Something Strange* some occasions when Albert assisted him in his investigations into the paranormal. Albert always spoke of how privileged he felt, and how much he valued the friendship of Archie – "A lovely man," he called him. Professor Roy has given me permission to reprint extracts from his book.

Window-shopping in the Mind

The average person is totally unaware that over the past century there has been collected an impressive body of evidence that certain human beings have the clairvoyant faculty, and ability to acquire data about people and places without using the normal five senses. Some of these clairvoyants, or sensitives, or paragnosts have been studied by careful and skilled psychical researchers who have had to come to the conclusion that their gift is genuine. One can be intellectually convinced of the reality of clairvoyance by the written evidence – one is gut-convinced by experiencing it for oneself.

Mr Albert Best, the well-known Glasgow medium, was introduced to me by a colleague, Professor John Macdonald, who took me to visit him at his home. My friend told me that he had not even given Mr Best my name or address. After some small talk, Mr Best, who accepts the spiritistic hypotheses to explain his results, told me that he had a number of people who had died and who wished to give me greetings and best wishes.

He asked: 'Does the name Smart mean anything to you?'

'Yes.'

'William Smart.'

'Yes.'

'I am getting the address 2, The University.'

I nodded.

'He is telling me to say to you, "You are following in my footsteps, aren't you?"'

Now Professor William Smart was Professor of Astronomy in Glasgow University. He lived in the Professors' Square at No. 2 The University. He wrote text-books and did research in celestial mechanics. He had three sons. He was one of my teachers when I was a student and I subsequently joined his department in 1957. Ultimately I became Professor of Astronomy at Glasgow University, wrote text-books, did research in celestial mechanics and had three sons. 'You are following in my footsteps, aren't you?' Just so.

The next ostensible communicator was a lady. Mr Best said her husband had been a master of works and his name was Bird. She sent her greetings. It meant nothing to me at the time and I said so. But later, when I returned to my office, something made me look at my old university diaries. It turned out that twenty years before, the university's master of works had been a Mr Bird. He was the last incumbent of that post; thereafter its name was changed to Superintendent of Fabric. I had had nothing to do with him and I could not think of any reason why he, let alone his wife, should wish to greet me.

Albert Best went on to other entities who evidently wished to greet me. He named them, gave me some characteristic details about each and also gave me the addresses they used to live at, complete to number and street name. All were in the vicinity of the address at which I now live. And yet I had never heard of most of them.

On making subsequent enquiries I found that these people had indeed existed and that they had lived at the addresses Mr Best had given me. In some cases, however, they had lived there ten years or more before I had moved to that district. The test was of course in no way conclusive but was certainly worth following up. I asked Mr Best if I could bring a friend to visit him in a fortnight's time. I was particularly careful in making this arrangement not only to avoid giving the name of the friend – I had at that time not even chosen which friend! – but also to avoid using the words 'he' or 'she'. When I took my friend to Mr Best's flat it was the first time he had met that person. I was of course careful not to introduce her to him. Mr Best, like a number of sensitives, goes into an almost imperceptible state of altered consciousness to operate. In that state. he claimed that my friend's father was present and that he was obtaining information from him. He made the following statements, though not in such rapid a manner. 'Your father is dead, your mother is still alive. You have one brother but no sisters. Your father was connected with the law. He died very suddenly. When reading and in his slippers he would place the heel of one on the toe of the other and had a habit of pushing the heel off his upper foot with the toe of the other slipper. His strongest drink was milk and it was a bit of a joke in the family. When you and your mother would try to persuade him to travel abroad he would say such things as "No, my heart's in the Highlands," and refuse to go. He had two watches. One is still in the family house, the other, a wristlet watch, has had a new watch strap put on it during the past week. I see you with a lot of other people. You are all writing, scribbling away. But you're not a novelist.'

Afterwards, my friend, who is a journalist and whose father was a police superintendent, confirmed that every single fact was correct, even to the watch which she happened to be wearing: it had belonged to her father and she had put a new strap on it a week previously.

There were at least twelve correct statements and no incorrect

Albert at Stansted Hall 1988

ones. Even if we say, quite unfairly, that the probability of any one of his statements being correct is as high as one-half, the overall probability of his performance being due to chance is less than one in 4000. In addition, however, he gave a number of other facts which he said were connected with my life and family. some of them going back thirty or more years. All were correct. If the two bodies of facts – 'mine' and 'my friend's'– had been switched one to the other, they would have lamentably failed to fit us. The whole experiment markedly strengthened my conviction that, whatever interpretation one makes of it, such a gift exists.

Built-in with the Bricks?

Council houses seem far more popular with ghosts these days than stately homes and castles as if comfort was a consideration in the psychic world. Certainly more of the cases I have been called out to have involved modem council houses than other habitation, a finding confirmed by my colleagues in psychical research.

Some years ago, in a little West of Scotland town, Max Magee and I had a case that perplexed us greatly for some time before the explanation, if explanation it was, presented itself to us. Max, Chaplain to Strathclyde University students, was called in by the Clerk to the Presbytery who knew of his experience in psychic matters. In his turn the Clerk had been consulted by the local minister of religion to whom the family concerned had fled for help.

On our first visit to the town, Max and I interviewed Mr and Mrs Wood. Peter was a pleasant young man, perhaps thirty years of age, his wife Karen a year or two younger. They had one child, Katie, a little girl of three. Both parents seemed sensible young people, though extremely worried ones when we saw them.

They had been very pleased to get their new council house. They were the first tenants and they had a lot of fun furnishing it and arranging things just as they wanted them. Katie had a little nursery along a short corridor from her parents' bedroom. Downstairs there was a very handsome lounge and a modern fitted kitchen.

The first phenomenon could be called 'the footsteps'. On a number of occasions the Woods, lying in bed at night, heard light quick footsteps coming along the corridor towards their room. When they first heard it, they thought Katie had somehow managed to get out of her cot and was coming to them.

But the bedroom door did not open and Karen, getting up and going to the nursery, found the little girl fast asleep. This happened several times before Karen stopped checking. She said to us 'We would lie listening to these footsteps and I would almost wish that something else would happen. In fact, one night when I was in the bath, I saw the door handle slowly move down and up. Peter denied that he was responsible and Katie was in her cot when it happened.'

On occasion, they said, visitors, sitting in the lounge downstairs, would hear the footsteps upstairs and make some remark like 'There isn't another child upstairs, is there?'

One evening, when Peter was away on business, Karen had put Katie to bed and was downstairs watching television in the lounge. She fell asleep to waken some time later with a start. She knew it must be very late for the TV screen showed the blizzard-like effect sometimes seen when the programmes have ended but the TV hadn't been switched off. With a feeling of dread, she saw, over by the fireplace, the tall dark figure of a woman dressed in black.

'And hating me,' said Karen. 'She didn't speak but she was resenting me. And I knew she wasn't real.'

'What did you do?' I asked.

'I don't know how I did it but I darted upstairs, got into bed and put my head under the bed clothes.'

The next time Peter went away on business, Karen invited

an old friend, a nursing sister from the Royal Infirmary, to stay the night. In the morning they found that each of them believed the other had got up in the middle of the night; half-aroused from sleep, they had seen a figure 'in a flowing negligee sort of gown' coming back to bed. Each denied getting up.

The final incident that drove the family from the house occurred when both parents were in bed. Shrieking with terror, their daughter rushed into their room, climbed on to the bed and burrowed in between them. It was a long time before they got her calmed down and got a coherent story out of her. She had found herself downstairs in the lounge where a 'monster' had attacked her and tried to choke her. She managed to break free and flee upstairs. Both parents tried to convince her that she had simply had a nasty dream. Both parents maintained however that their daughter was not given to nightmares. In any event the child's terror, together with the other incidents, communicated itself to them and they felt unable to stay in the house.

There are quite a few reasons other than the paranormal why a house is alleged to be haunted. The tenants may want to be re-housed to a better habitation or a more salubrious neighbourhood and, in the absence of any of the more ordinary ways of persuading the authorities to carry out their wishes, pretend that their house is haunted. Or there may be physical, natural phenomena, unrecognised as such, that lead the family to a genuine belief that they are the target of mischievous or malevolent spirits. Houses creak and trains of raps can occur when there is a change in temperature, especially if the house is old. Sounds travel and can result in whispers being heard that actually originate in an adjoining dwelling. A water hammer – an airlock in the plumbing – can alarm the family by a sudden peremptory loud series of booming sounds, to be transformed into a poltergeist by the family which has just been watching *The Amityville Horror* or *The Exorcist* on TV.

And, of course, there are those unfortunates, mentally disturbed people whose delusions take the form of believing that aliens are beaming death-rays at them, or that the Devil is living in their cellar, waiting to get them, or that they are haunted.

In the case of the Woods, none of the usual normal reasons seemed to apply. We therefore decided to pay a visit to the house, this time accompanied by Mr Albert Best the well-known Glasgow medium whom we both knew and who we both believed had a genuine psychic gift. Without telling him where we were going, or anything about the case other than that a young couple seemed to need our help, we drove to the Woods' house. Peter Wood was present when we entered the house.

In such cases Albert Best finds it useful to wander about the house, waiting for impressions to come to him. He interprets these impressions in a frankly spiritualistic way. Ascending the inside stairs of the house, Albert walked slowly along the short corridor then stopped. He seemed to listen for a while before speaking. 'Children. There are children here. They come from the other side. They like to come here. It's a good loving atmosphere here so they like to come and play here.'

We went downstairs. In the lounge he halted, looking fixedly towards the massive fireplace, a handsome feature of the room built of genuine stones, and rubbed his hands together as if cold.

'Oh, it's different here. There's a woman over there. By the fireplace. An old woman. She sees us. And she doesn't like us. She's confused. She's saying 'What are all these young people doing in my house?''

Peter Wood watched and listened in obvious bewilderment and scepticism. 'But no-one has stayed in this house apart from us. We're the first family here.' Albert nodded. He walked across to the fireplace and paused. 'I'll try to get some more information.'

Albert Best as a medium is noted for the accuracy of names and addresses he obtains, unlike many other mediums, who, although they may have a genuine psychic gift, find it difficult to get names and addresses. It is possible that Albert is good at this because for many years he was a postman in Northern Ireland and may have become conditioned into associating names with addresses.

'I get the name Baird Street.'

Peter Wood said 'That's where we got the stones.'

It turned out that Peter and his father-in-law had built the handsome fireplace in the lounge, bringing the stones it was built of from a demolished cottage in Baird Street, on the outskirts of the town. The big stone over the fire itself had been the lintel of a window in the cottage. Albert turned his attention elsewhere again. After a while he said "I've finally managed to get through to her. She didn't know she's dead. She was ill for a long time before she passed over and in her confused state still thought she was in her own cottage. She couldn't understand why she was seeing strangers in her house. She's very sorry for the trouble she's caused and apologises. I've shown her how she can move on and she says there'll be no further trouble."

Spiritualism of course teaches that we survive death and that some of us can get 'stuck' on the other side for one reason or another. I've come across a number of cases where such a hypotheses has to be taken seriously. Karl Wickland subscribed to this theory. So does Edwin Butler. On the other hand there is also the psychometrist theory. It is the case that there are certain gifted people who, given an object belonging to someone else, achieve some kind of strange rapport with that person be he or she living or dead. The psychometrist is then able to reel off all kinds of facts regarding that person's past, present and immediate future. The rapport can be so strong that the psychometrist not only seems to have that person present but can take on, or be 'overshadowed' by, the physical and mental characteristics and idiosyncrasies of that person. The stones Peter and his father-in-law had used to build the fireplace had come from the ruined cottage. Did they act as 'objects' in the psychometrist theory, enabling Albert to enter into rapport with a former owner of the cottage? Or is it true that some of us become, on the other side of death, 'Earthbound', in the Spiritualist term, destined to hang around in a confused, dreamlike state, bewildered by a mixture of data perceived from two levels of being, impinging at times in a troublesome way on this facet of reality?

It would be nice to be able to say that Albert's intervention solved the problem. It would have tied the case up neatly. Certainly the family were encouraged by this 'explanation' to return to the council house and certainly the old lady was never seen again, which was consistent with the hypothesis that her Earth-bound shade or spirit or whatever had been built in with the bricks, so to speak, and subsequently released by Albert.

On the other hand, some phenomena were reported to us thereafter by Mr and Mrs Woods. On one occasion they returned to the house one evening and found that all the drawers in their bedroom had been removed from the dressing table and wardrobe and laid neatly on the floor. Nothing was missing.

On other occasions a dog was seen running upstairs in the house, a number of different people catching glimpses of the animal. No dog was found upstairs. Another of the strange happenings of the time involved a conviction of Karen Woods as she lay in bed, that on some nights there was a presence in the bed with her and Peter that gripped her ankles. In spite of such phenomena. real or fancied, however, the Woods family remained in their council house and quite soon, as often happens, no further phenomena were reported.

Albert and Mary Duffy at the annual seminar,
Kilmarnock SNU Church 1993

8

Giving and Receiving

Albert became friendly with the Rev. David Kennedy after the passing of his wife, and it was through Albert's mediumship that David became convinced of survival beyond the grave. He subsequently wrote a best-selling book entitled *A Venture in Immortality* detailing the extraordinary evidence he received through Albert. The Rev. Kennedy, a Minister of the Church of Scotland, addressed many meetings and services at which Albert was demonstrating his mediumship.

Psychic News of November 1975 reports:

Chief Rabbi returns

The Rev. David Kennedy, whom I met with his wife the day after his brilliant speech at the Royal Albert Hall reunion service, told me of an intriguing spirit message he received a fortnight earlier.

It came through Albert Best, who was responsible for so many evidential communications from Ann, David's first wife. The medium said she was accompanied by famous film star Leslie Howard, who had previously been described to David. On earth Ann had done a sketch of him. The intriguing communication, which he asked me to confirm, came from one who said he was Joseph German Hertz, had been a Chief Rabbi and gave the East London address where he lived. Dr Hertz, I found, was Chief Rabbi from 1913 to his passing in 1946.

It took hours to check that Rose Freed, his wife's first two names, were also correctly given by the medium.

This led me to tell David and Shirley the story of a remarkable spirit message featuring a rabbi which I received through Robin Stevens.

The extraordinary thing was the medium's statement that I could confirm from his son, whose name he gave as Bronkhorst, that he had a glass eye. This proved correct.

As I related this story, David excitedly interrupted me to say Best had said he would hear a story about a rabbi with a glass eye when he came to London! An added point is that one of this rabbi's sons now works for PN.

Another Minister of the Church of Scotland, the Rev. Donald MacKay, also spoke at many of Albert's demonstrations, and he and his wife Maime became very dear friends of Albert.

Perhaps one of the greatest inspirations to Albert, who continuously gave of his gifts and himself, came from his experiences in Physical Home Circles of years before. In 1979 in *Psychic News*, Albert praised the Glasgow Physical Medium, Edith Hall, at the time of her transition:

"My 'dead' mother kissed me"

Glasgow's leading medium Albert Best tells of a dramatic seance at which his mother materialised and embraced him. He does so in reporting the passing of Edith Hall, one of Glasgow's last physical mediums. She demonstrated her mediumship for over forty years.

Albert says "I was privileged to witness some of her wonderful phenomena. I was embraced by loved ones and guides on many occasions."

Voices were identified.

Once about twelve solid spirit hands "tried to lift me off a chair. As they did so, the communicators sang, 'Fare ye well Inniskillins' ."

These were some of his wartime comrades whose earthly lives ended in the North African campaign.

Albert recognised their voices, particularly the rich Tipperary brogue of one they called Coffer. This unusual nickname was supplied at the seance. "It is the only name by which I knew him."

Another time, Albert's mother, whom he did not know on earth, "came forward and kissed me. We spoke of personal things nobody else knew about. She stood in the middle of the room and sang in Irish Gaelic 'Believe me if all those endearing young charms.' The reunion with my family is too personal and precious to talk about."

Albert was also present when a young man, a rent collector who, the previous week, had been tortured and stabbed returned. "He implored me to tell his wife he was all right."

The guides' singing, he said could be heard quite a distance away.

"I knew most of these wonderful mediums, like John Sloan. Mary McCallin and Alex Martin. They sat for development ten to twelve years, keeping gifts unsoiled and unsullied. Their faith in God and the spirit world was never shaken. I wonder how many today have the patience to sit for so long? Mrs Hall has gone to join her husband and reap the benefits of all those years of service."

The following extract is taken from an interview given by Albert to a *Psychic News* Reporter in January 1972:

He embraced his materialised wife and three children

I heard last week the fascinating psychic story of a medium who has held his fully-materialised 'dead' wife and children in his arms and shaken hands with his guides.

He is the well-known non-professional Glasgow medium, Albert Best who, for 28 of his 53 years, has served Spiritualism with dedicated devotion. The result is a well-deserved splendid reputation for his versatile mediumship.

Albert and Rosalind at Stansted 1993

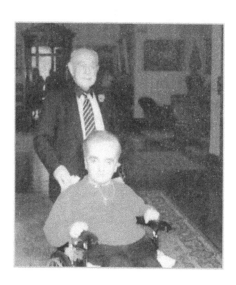

*Albert and Ronnie
at Stansted 1993*

Ever since his London debut at Acacia House, Acton, in 1968, I have tried without success to interview him for a profile article. I finally tied down this most diffident medium to a lunch hour appointment during his visit last week to the College of Psychic Studies.

As he had many friends there, Albert decided to settle in Glasgow. The double-Celt psychic, who reminds me of a benign gnome, has spent more time there than in his native Ireland. "I would not choose to live anywhere else," he said. In Ayr and Glasgow he experienced memorable physical phenomena at private home circles. The first was with Alec Martin of Ayr, who passed on several years ago.

Albert had the joy of holding in his arms the fully-materialised forms of Rose and his three children.

I thought it strange he has never contacted them through his own mediumship. "I don't wish to," said Albert.

His spirit guides have also materialised and shaken hands with him.

Albert showed me bullet scars in his neck and left arm resulting from an injury for which he has a small army disability pension. He also draws a Civil Service pension.

After watching Albert demonstrate first-class clairvoyance at Acacia House last Saturday, I deplore his reticence. He regards this gift as secondary to his healing for which he holds three weekly sessions in Glasgow.

Anyone like myself who had the privilege of knowing Albert socially, must have frequently been enthralled with his stories of the great gifts of other Mediums which he had witnessed.

Typical of Albert – he was always ready to give credit to others where due.

9

Tributes from some Colleagues

Mary Duffy, that excellent medium from Edinburgh, shared a special friendship with Albert over a period of more than thirty years. She says that her first experience of working with him was at an evening of clairvoyant demonstration after an SNU AGM held in Langside Halls, Glasgow, which she found terrifying and where hundreds of people were present. She remembers Albert was very encouraging and she will never forget his kindness. From that time onwards they frequently shared the platform. She comments that Albert said very little about where he went and what he did, and he was always very discreet about the work he did behind the scenes with the unfortunate souls who suffered from drug and alcohol addiction.

Very many people to whom he gave healing have cause to be grateful for his gift. She knows Albert will be remembered in many countries as well as Great Britain with a great deal of love and admiration for his dedication, and also for the help he gave to the younger mediums just starting out. She will always be proud to have been considered by him a friend.

A tribute to Albert from Ivy Scott, a lovely lady and brilliant medium who is now in her ninety-sixth year and still working for Spirit:

The Albert I know – one of Nature's Gentlemen.

"As a Medium he needed no blazing trumpets, his work spoke for itself all over many different countries. His love of his work and concern for the people to whom it brought comfort, was as natural as breathing. I remember the man himself – so very human in every way.

Never puffed up with his success. A very sensitive man. He had a natural sense of fun and enjoyment, yet even in the midst of a party could spare a thought for anyone he realised needed help. The first time Albert and I met was at the College of Psychic Studies. We both had work to do that day and as I was waiting in the Reception Room for my appointments he came over to me and said 'We have never met, but can you understand the name Geoffrey spelt with a G?' I said 'Yes, indeed I can.'

'Well he is there beside you sending you such care and love. He is about twenty-years-old and I just had to tell you.'

Before I could answer Albert was called away, but I was both thrilled and amazed, for we had lost our son just a year ago to that day. Albert was also very helpful in such an unobtrusive manner. He would give you the moon if he could reach it, and ask nothing in return. When I was ill and unable to work he put channels in operation that helped me enormously, yet he expected no thanks.

It was an honour and a pleasure to work with him at Pembridge. There was always a sense of comradeship and never any rivalry. A lady one evening after our double demonstration came to me to say good night and I quote: 'I have enjoyed tonight. I did not receive a message, but it was a pleasure to listen to you both. You work so differently, yet you complement each other.' That's the real Albert."

Ivor James, talented musician, artist and himself a man with many spiritual gifts, writes:

"Any Theatrical Casting Director would have had him marked down for the part of a genial landlord of a local hostelry or perhaps a gentleman farmer, but as a Spiritualist Medium NO, which only goes to show appearances are not everything. Not only was Albert Best in truth a Spiritual Medium, but certainly one of the best of his time. I never did get to know him all that well, but on the few occasions when we did meet I always came away feeling uplifted. His attitude to Spiritualism was anything but orthodox, which I can illustrate by telling you something which he once said to me, at Stansted Hall no less. 'Spiritualism,' he said, 'I love very dearly, but Spiritualists frighten me to death.' They don't make them like that anymore!

I am sure that wherever there are gatherings of Spiritually minded people in the next life, there Albert will be, with a glass of ambrosia and a cigarette in his hand, radiating his own particular brand of love and joy, and all the time believing that he himself is 'no great shakes'. How wrong can you be, Albert?"

Don Galloway recalls the following incident:

"I had never met Albert until he came to work for us at the College of Psychic Studies, and on his first visit we managed to arrange for him to stay with a College member in Kensington, this being in 1970. Needless to say, his schedule of sittings at the College was booked up solidly for weeks before his arrival but in the middle of the week a sitter had to cancel at the very last minute, so rather than have Albert hanging around with nothing to do, I quickly went to his room and took the sitting myself. He was one of the extremely few mediums ever to make contact with my fiancée who had died suddenly many years before, and he also gave me good evidence of the closeness of a couple of my relatives and old college friends. However, he insisted I should remember one important thing from there onwards – 'Always remember corruption starts at the top, and never forget it.' This puzzled me then. I thought it a rather strange thing for anyone in Spirit to be telling me. However, not very long after this I had my first proofs of the value of this caution, and right where I would have least expected to find it.

Do I have to add that, of course, I have seen it proven many times since, and again where it should least be expected?

What eventually proved to be most striking, though, was when Albert told me of a gentleman of the name Mowbray contacting us, saying he was interested in the work I was then doing, but most keen to help me in the greater work yet to be done, touring the world and also writing about matters of the Spirit. At the time I had no idea who this man could be, and had neither the desire nor intention to work in the ways in which he expressed interest. Albert said that Mr Mowbray would, in course of time, prove in an unexpected way, that he had been with us at this sitting and that he was following up his interest in my work.

Some four years later, by then away from the College and, through Spirit direction, touring the world in their name, a certain amount of publicity regarding my travels brought forth some very interesting letters, the most striking of which from a lady I'd never heard of, enclosing some genuine Spirit photographs of years ago, and saying that she felt impressed by her father in Spirit to send these to me from his old research collection, as I might at some time need to show and refer to them in my future work. The lady's name was Miss Stella Mowbray.

Dear Albert – medium supreme – and a most loving and truly gentle gentleman! Bless him."

Don also recalls:

"Albert the not so Perfect Sitter!"

"It was in 1971 when Albert, in London to work with us at the College of Psychic Studies. stayed a few days at my home in Chiswick. Shortly before this we had each, separately, met with an American couple at a *Psychic News* Dinner-Dance, who had told us of their twelve-year-old daughter developing her physical mediumship. They had invited us for an evening to the luxury flat they had rented in Bayswater, when, with some other leading figures in Spiritualism. their daughter was to give a Materialisation Seance. Not being too concerned with physical mediumship myself, I had politely declined the invitation, but Albert, whilst staying with me, just casually announced that he had promised I would attend this affair with him.

Need I say, we both had strong reservations about what might develop with this supposed twelve-year-old physical medium and we were astonished to find that before the séance all the guests were invited to enjoy many kinds of drinks and cocktail snacks. This before an apparent Trance and Materialisation seance indeed! Never having been much of a drinker myself. I settled for fruit juices and was amazed that Albert, who never, ever drank at all before going into any form of mediumistic work, either his own or to sit for the development of another, knocked back two or three scotches! (Later this was proved to be not so much amazing as plain, darned clever!)

All settled eventually, about sixteen or eighteen of us in the large lounge, curtains drawn, only the dimmest light on. We had to meditate a few moments before the 'medium' came in, and when she did we were all welcomed by the supposedly entranced girl in not so much pidgin-English as pidgin-American! The meditation period had served Albert particularly well – the perfect reason for dozing off, this later to be translated into 'having gone under deep control'! He never awoke at all and in the course of a whole lot of absolute nonsense as the girl moved around the circle I suddenly found her sitting on me and telling me how delighted she was I had come because I was her favourite blue-eyed pin-up! Need I say how desperately I wished I could curl up and somehow vanish through the floor.

Addressing me as Donsie-Babe, she spoke in the most sickening kiddy-tone I think I've ever had to contend with. However, when getting around to the one she called 'Uncle Albie' she had no response whatsoever, and then,with a giggle, checked herself, saying, 'Oh, I forgot, I'm not supposed to disturb old people when they're resting!'

I could hardly wait to be on the way home to inform Albert he was now an old person needing his rest. He would then be fifty-four! I was even more astonished when, on our eventual departure, the precocious child's mother thanked Albert for giving out so much power to the circle in his 'trance', and I never even got thanked for having kept awake and attentive, and staying the whole course! Dear Albert!"

From Stewart Lawson, a wonderful medium now living in South Africa:

"I feel very touched at being asked to add a few words with regard to Albert. I spent some very happy moments in his company and enjoyed his conversation on various experiences which he recalled with great humour. When Albert and Ivor Davies got together it was always a wonderful evening. You see I first met Albert at Edward Street Church in Brighton and always admired his work and looked upon him as a good ambassador for the World of Spirit. I loved his outrageous stories, all of which were true.

On Albert's visits to South Africa, which we all looked forward to, he always brought a breath of home (England) to many of us out here. It is funny, but I never had the joy of sharing a platform with him, but to have known him and shared in his life was something I will always remember and am grateful for. When I first saw him sitting on the platform, I thought he looked like a little elf. I felt he should be repairing shoes, but one thing is for certain – he was used to repair many broken hearts. Lots of love Albert, and God Bless."

Stewart Lawson.

From Charles Sherratt in Cape Town:

"How can anyone describe someone like Albert Best in the cold hard print of this world? He who was so very often somewhere between the two worlds, working to unite loved ones who had been parted by what is known as death.

To those who came into contact with him in such circumstances, he was sympathy, understanding and compassion all rolled into one. During my almost twenty years as General Manager of Stansted Hall, I was privy to much that he did to help people in his own way. I well remember one such case in the early 80s. Albert was at the College for a week and on his arrival he mentioned to me that he was expecting visitors on the Sunday afternoon, and would I be kind enough to make the Blue room available and provide some little refreshment at about 3.30 pm when all the students would be in a lecture. I was in Reception just before 3.00 pm, in time to see a large black Rolls-Royce drive up, complete with liveried chauffeur, and I opened the door of the Hall to admit two ladies (who shall remain nameless) and a little boy of about six or seven.

I showed them in to meet Albert, and at about 3.30 pm I took a tray of tea in for them. I had included a large glass of orange juice for the little boy. I served the tea and offered the tray, with the cold drink on it, to the little boy – I was suddenly aware that the ladies and Albert were watching to see what the boy would do and as he picked up the glass with his right hand the youngest of the ladies (his mother) burst into tears.

Albert saw them off some little time later and I then asked him what it was all about? The ladies had brought the little boy to Albert for healing – he had been unable to fully use his right hand since birth and, today, he had picked up a full glass of orange juice with that hand, unaided. Just one of the many instances of Spirit working through Albert Best.

One other remarkable instance, this time of Albert's mediumship!

On the 25th anniversary of the opening of the College, we had a large exhibition and a whole series of events, all of which were well advertised and attended. Albert was the Demonstrator at the opening ceremony, and for some time before we had had quite a lot of trouble with a young man who had come with a coach party from London. He had been drinking, having brought his own supply with him, and when Albert began to demonstrate he became quite abusive. Albert tried to calm him down and we tried to get at him to remove him but he was in the middle of the audience. The young man made some sarcastic remark about mediumship and mediums in general – quick as a flash, Albert shouted at him, 'I have your mother here with me, and she tells me that you have only just ceased to be a 'Guest of Her Majesty', and that she is disgusted with your behaviour.' The young man looked as if he had been struck, he screamed something and ran from the College grounds and we never saw him again.

Albert Best, wherever he is now, will still be the same kind and understanding man he was in this world, a man who lived what he believed and who I will always think of with love and affection, as a gentle man in word and deed. Much love, Albert."

Charles Sherratt.

Tribute to Albert Best - Leah Bond:

"It was in the year of 1971 that I attended a small Spiritualist Chapel situated in the Rhondda Valley of South Wales. One particular evening there was an announcement that renowned medium Albert Best would be touring South Wales and would be demonstrating at a local Chapel at Porth. There was great excitement when everyone clambered to buy tickets for the Special Venue. I got caught up in the rush and bought two tickets, one for my mother and one for myself. I did not have a clue who Albert Best was but he was 'from away' and as far as Scotland so he had to be worth a look.

My mother and I attended the meeting and I was surprised to see this small stocky man climb up to the pulpit. Rather unassuming and ordinary, not at all what I expected. The hymns were sung and the rafters rang which produced a wonderful energy that Welsh people, crammed packed into a Baptist Chapel (hired for the special event), could bring about. Albert proceeded with his demonstration and astounded everyone with his evidence of survival. He eventually linked with my mother. At this point I wish to state to the reader that women from the valleys of South Wales and the people who know the courage of miners' wives will understand that my mother had seen many hard times and equally many tragedies in her life. She was not, therefore, prone to easy tears – in fact I don't think I can recall ever seeing my mother cry. She was of the character 'stiff upper lip' and 'take life on the chin' so to speak.

Albert brought wonderful evidence to my mother and she was moved to tears. Later, on the way home to her little village I saw, out of the comer of my eye, how she was still wiping her eyes. The message and evidence given was for my mother and now that she is in Spirit I will not open up the personal contents. However, this much I can say, when she got out of the car she turned to me and said with such sincerity and conviction:

'Leah! that man Albert Best walks with God because only God and myself know the events he spoke of and described tonight.' My mother was never easily moved and never gave credit unless it was due. Bearing this in mind I continued to admire and respect this small ordinary man with such a huge extraordinary gift of attunement with God and Spirit.

Many years passed by and I also followed along the pathway of mediumship, always remembering and hoping to achieve the same kind of attunement as my hero 'Albert Best'. I am still trying and hoping to this day.

My Spiritual pathway brought me into touch with Don Galloway of Lynwood Fellowship and at this point I give my thanks to Don for his encouragement in my endeavours of my mediumship.

One day I had a phone call from Don who enquired if I would be available to work at Stansted Hall. After taking a few great gulps I confirmed I would venture forward and try my best. Don then said I would receive a letter in a few days from a lady in London – Ros Cattanach. Ros has since become a friend and another great help to me when working at the London Spiritual Mission. I received the letter from Ros who enclosed a copy of the week's Venue at Stansted Hall and lo and behold the week was 'Albert Best's week'. You could have knocked me down with a feather. I felt I had come up on the 'Spiritual Lottery'.

I later found out that this was to be Albert's last organised week at Stansted. Coincidence, friends? No way! Motivated for me by that wonderful Spiritual Mechanism. This happened in the year 1994. I set off to Stansted Hall with great trepidation and excitement and was even more pleased to find I was actually sitting next to Albert at meal times. Also bowled over to find I would actually share a platform with him – my hero who had had such an effect on my 'hard as a nut' mother all those years ago.

The week came to an end all too soon but before I departed I was invited to work 'Yuletide Week' at Stansted 1994. I accepted and when that time came I arrived at Stansted Hall not knowing who my fellow workers would be and again a little apprehensive. However, to my delight Albert had unexpectedly decided to spend Xmas at the Hall and had flown down that day from Scotland. Yet another Bonus from Spirit. Again we shared the same seating arrangements at mealtimes and on Xmas morning at breakfast Albert gave me a wink and said there was a 'little something' under my plate for me. I found a small plastic card with a verse which read as follows:

Believe In Yourself

If you think you are beaten,
You are:
If you think you dare not,
You don't.
If you'd like to win, but think you can't,
It's almost a cinch you won't.
If you think you'll lose, you're lost,
For out in the world we find ....
Success begins with
A fellow's will:
It's all in a state of mind.
Life's battles don't always go
To the stronger or faster man:
But soon or late
The man who wins
Is the one who thinks
He can!

I was so thrilled to receive a little keepsake and have cherished that card to this day. I carry it with me at all times. Again the week passed all too quickly and it was time to depart for New Year 1995. I said my farewell to Albert in the reception area but for some reason kept having to come back into the area at least half a dozen times. I felt I did not want to leave Albert. I remember saying to a lady from Stourbridge, 'I am loathe to leave Albert because I feel I won't see him in this world again.' This turned out to be very true.

The following spring of 1995 it was necessary for me to seek advice from a Specialist Consultant about my health. After an exploratory operation I was diagnosed with cancer. I was told I had three to six months to sort out my affairs. I immediately thought of the first line of the little poem Albert had given me: "If you think you are beaten – You are" and I informed the Specialist categorically – NO WAY!! I have work to do and

I intend to be here until I am at least ninety. Major surgery followed on May 11th 1995 followed by three weeks' treatment at the Welsh Cancer Hospital in Cardiff. At this time, I kept reading Albert's poem and taking strength from the fact that he had been inspired to give it to me for this challenging time and to make me know that Spirit would help me through.

This was supported from Spirit by another leading light Gee Summay, Spiritual Mother of Lynwood Fellowship. My links with Lynwood Fellowship and Albert Best pulled me through and helped me to stay on Mother Earth to continue my Spiritual work.

The final tribute I must share with you is from Albert in the Spirit World. Again I had decided to take a welcome break at Stansted Hall on the 'Lynwood Fellowship Week'. Among the mediums on the programme was Gordon Smith from Scotland. I was told he had been encouraged and inspired in his mediumship by Albert. I made a pact with Albert that if I had a sitting with Gordon Smith I expected him to turn up with some evidence or else! I went along to the sitting and was greeted by a very nice and affable young man. Gordon proceeded to give me very good evidence which I could accept but was not what I was after. Then about ten minutes into the sitting Gordon said, 'Hang on! Albert Best has just arrived and wishes to be remembered to you. He states you know him and that you also worked for him and shared a platform with him.'

Incidentally Gordon Smith had never met me before and had no inkling of any connection between Albert and myself. The sitting proceeded with further evidence of excellent quality and we parted happily saying we would try and get together during the week, to talk about our mutual friend Albert.

During that week I joined some friends at Hitchin Spiritualist Church on a day trip to the 'Royal Stuart' factory at Stourbridge. Walking around the factory shop I saw a small crystal bowl with a thistle engraved on the inside of the bowl. I thought to myself,

'I'll buy that, Albert, to commemorate such an evidential message in my sitting with Gordon Smith.' I walked farther along and saw a lovely Waterford crystal picture frame which I fell in love with. I stood holding the bowl in one hand and the picture frame in the other and felt to buy both would be extravagant. Whilst pondering I heard Albert's strong Celtic voice say 'Give the bowl to Gordon.' It was so distinct and clear I nearly dropped both items. These were boxed and packed for me, each being reminders of Albert, since I later discovered he was Irish not Scottish and Waterford crystal comes from Ireland. Arriving back at Stansted Hall I was somewhat embarrassed presenting a gift to Gordon, who later that day came looking for me and told me this story –

When Albert was on earth he had bought Gordon and his family the same Royal Stuart bowl but unfortunately one of Gordon's small children had accidentally broken this. Gordon was naturally upset because Albert had bought the bowl as a token of friendship to the family. Albert from Spirit must have been very aware of Gordon's disappointment and had used my visit to the Royal Stuart factory to replace the same bowl.

It is heart-warming to have sure realisation that life continues and that given the opportunity and co-operation our loved ones can prove to us that they are still very much a part of our lives. Blessings to you, Albert, friend and fellow worker for those Spirit Realms. May your light and laughter continue to shine in your special part of the Universe. – Hello? was that the chink of a whisky glass I hear?

NO!! It was Albert just adjusting his well-earned Angel wings."

10

They meet again

Christine Peebles records her introduction to Albert and Spiritualism:

"March 9th 1988, my brother, Brian aged 28, died in a house fire. This was to be the most profound and painful event in my life, and as it transpired, an event that would affect one of my best friends in an extraordinary way. My brother's passing devastated me. We had a close, loving relationship and I simply could not imagine continuing in this world without him.

I was 23 years old and worked in a hairdresser's with Gordon Smith. I had known Gordon for about ten years. He was a good friend. Gordon felt my pain and desperately wanted to help me. Gordon asked me if there was anything that he could do. I had heard about Spiritualism, but had very little knowledge about it, neither had Gordon at that time. In answer to his question I asked him to find a Spiritualist Church and take me there.

On 13th March, the day after Brian's funeral, Gordon took me and my brother's girlfriend Fiona, to a Church in Somerset Place. The three of us sat in the front row, the medium was a woman called Mary Duffy. We were the first to be approached by Mary. She described my mother's passing, my mum told her to tell me that I would have the strength to get through my recent bereavement. As can be imagined I was distraught and very emotional, Mary was understanding and kind. After the service we approached Mary, asking her for the impossible. I wanted her to tell me exactly where my brother was, what he was feeling, what he was doing ... had he suffered? Again, Mary was gentle. She explained that it was too soon, Brian would be going through a process of healing, helping him to accept and adjust to his new environment. Mary advised me to try to see a man called Albert Best, she described him as one of the best mediums in Britain, she assured me that if anyone could answer my many questions it would be Mr Best.

After the service Gordon, Fiona and I discussed what we had been told and took comfort from the new knowledge we had been given ... that there was life after death. Gordon was intrigued and talked about this man who had been recommended, Mr Best. We resolved that if we had the opportunity we would go to see this man.

Well, we waited a long time, I waited longer than Gordon. It was 1992, early April. I was again embroiled in another tragedy. My friend, Stewart aged twenty-five, was dying of AIDS. I was spending all my free time with him, trying to smooth his passing in whatever way I could. Gordon telephoned me one Sunday morning, he had been to Somerset Place the previous night, the medium was Mr Albert Best.

Mr Best had asked the audience if there was anyone who knew of someone on the earth plane who was dying of AIDS.

After a few minutes, Gordon reluctantly put his hand up (reluctantly because he did not know Stewart personally).

Incredibly Mr Best went on to describe my brother to Gordon; a young man who had passed in tragic circumstances, a fire, he had worked in the theatre. He also said that the young man would not give his name, but that this was simply a trait of his personality. He was also able to say that this was the man's first communication from the higher side of life, all of which was true. Brian was quiet and deep, not a great conversationalist.

Mr Best told Gordon that this message was not intended for him personally and should be passed to someone he knew, the sister of the young man communicating with him. Mr Best went on to say that my brother was watching over Stewart and that

Stewart would pass before the last day of the present month.

Stewart passed on 29th April. A great deal of comfort was gained by many people from the message from my brother relayed by Mr Best... and wasn't it strange that the first medium to give definite proof of my brother's continued existence was the very man recommended to us four years previously.

During the preceding four years Gordon's development and progression as a medium was phenomenal, he was rapidly becoming respected throughout Glasgow and soon Britain. After his message in Somerset Place, Gordon struck up a strong lasting friendship with Mr Best, but I still had not met the man, despite hearing so much about him. One Sunday night after a long drive I arrived home at around 10 pm. I had been visiting relatives in Kintyre. I had just put my bags down when I decided that I wanted to speak to Gordon. I telephoned him at his home. Gordon immediately said that he felt that I should go to his house. I protested, saying that I was tired, but Gordon was insistent. I became intrigued and agreed, I could be there in ten minutes.

On my arrival Gordon answered the door, he told me that Mr Best was there and had apparently been picking up impressions Gordon felt sure related to my brother. Gordon gave me his assurance that none of the company had mentioned me or had given Mr Best any information. With some trepidation I ventured into the sitting room and there was Mr Albert Best sitting in an armchair relaxed and comfortable, enjoying the company. My first impression was that he was pretty ordinary. He was quite short, had white hair which was a little thin on top, he had a lovely smile that lit up his face and lent a mischievous twinkle to his eyes.

As I said, my first impression was that he was 'ordinary', that did not last long. Soon after my arrival I walked towards an alcove behind Mr Best's chair, he immediately started sniffing the air, he looked at me and said that he could smell smoke (no one else in the room could smell anything unusual). Not wanting to offer information, I returned Mr Best's gaze, he then said that the smoke was in connection with a young man who had passed suddenly and that this man was here for me ... !

Over the course of the evening Mr Best offered me astonishing personal proof, he also confirmed that Stewart, the boy who died of AIDS, was with Brian. It was an emotional evening and one I will not forget. The link between Mr Best and my brother seems to have come full circle.

I was contacted by Gordon in January 1998, he explained to me that he had been with a well-known medium, while with her she began to relay a message to him; he was able to identify that it was Mr Albert Best communicating with him. Part of his message was once again intended for my ears, Mr Best wanted Gordon to let me know that he is now with the young man.

Thank you, Albert."

Ann Docherty and Gordon Smith at Albert's Thanksgiving Service at Berkeley Street Church, 1996

11
Happy Memories

Some of my happiest memories of Albert are from his weeks at Stansted Hall. Albert knew both John and Arthur Findlay and his wife for some years, often staying at their home, before Arthur's passing in 1964 when he bequeathed his house to the Spiritualist National Union to create a centre for studies in the Spiritual Sciences.

Apart from spending some weeks at the college as a guest of other mediums, Albert always had one week in each year – usually the second week in July – when he invited other mediums and healers to join him. This was a most popular week for guests, always fully booked and usually with a waiting list in case of cancellation. Friends came from many countries and regulars from all parts of the United Kingdom.

Albert loved Stansted and thrived amongst the company of old friends, his face alight with pleasure as he greeted them and welcomed newcomers. Until the last few years he used to rise very early and he and I would wander around the grounds amongst the trees soon after 6am.

Good programmes were presented, a variety of interesting lectures, discussion groups and private sittings, together with healing available all through the day with excellent healers. Evening entertainment was usually in a lighter vein and very popular. and the Public Services with a good speaker and Albert demonstrating were packed. At that time the word 'tutoring' had not become the criterion at Stansted, but most guests left at the end of Albert's week with increased knowledge and love of the Spirit, many booking for the following year before they departed!

Albert had a great affinity with children, animals and all forms of nature, particularly trees. Every year he held one meditation session in the sanctuary, always on trees, and most visitors would never miss this. Albert frequently was asked to conduct Naming Ceremonies in the sanctuary and this to me and to many others, was a most moving experience. His love really shone through when he took a small child in his arms and those joining in the ceremony were often visibly emotionally affected.

On the last night of the week the inevitable Concert was produced. For a few years a sketch was written around our friend Albert and this was certainly the high spot of the evening. Albert appeared as Prince Charming in *Cinderella* with Cinders and two Ugly Sisters – The Sheik of Araby with two ladies from his harem – Albert Doolittle in *My Fair Lady* with Eliza and Professor Higgins. He also acted in a sketch as an elf, singing "I'm shy, Mary Ellen, I'm shy" with two fairies, and this brought down the house. There were other performances and how he loved playing the fool – fluffed his lines; the witty script often unheard due to the roars of laughter at this buffoonery – the crowning glory being one year when his trousers fell down as he left the stage!

Whilst Albert did not join the healers because of his other commitments, very occasionally he was asked to give healing to someone in great need, often a child. This was never done in public, only with one or two close friends whom he chose to be with him. He usually went into deep trance and Dr Wong worked through him. A very wonderful experience for anyone who was privileged to witness this healing.

Albert had his last week at the Hall in 1994 as he felt strongly it was time for him to retire from this activity, but he was invited to the Stourbridge week in 1995 by Eric Hatton, who one evening produced "This is your Life, Albert Best" in the sanctuary. Albert and all the guests, with the exception of two or three who participated, were completely taken by surprise. Albert, after the initial shock, became his usual ebullient self, causing much laughter by his remarks, although it was obvious at times he was deeply moved at the tributes paid. An evening not to be forgotten.

What weeks those were. The atmosphere of love, friendship and joy abounded throughout. Albert was feted, cosseted and loved by all his friends, but his natural humility and lack of self-importance kept his feet firmly on the ground and he never became big-headed or suffered an inflated ego. I am sure many of us will say 'those were the days!'

Albert said on many occasions if it were not for his gift of mediumship people wouldn't bother with him. How wrong he was; those of us who knew him liked and loved the man himself. His warmth and kindliness shone through, and his generosity knew no bounds. His greatest joy was giving, buying 'wee presents' for his friends and arriving home from trips abroad with a case filled with gifts.

Albert had a true sense of humour as he had the ability to laugh at himself, and he told many tales of the stupid things he had done from time to time. I am sure there are many people with whom he has stayed who could relate laughable incidents which occurred whilst he was with them. He usually stayed with my husband and me two or three times a year and we loved having him. There was never a dull moment! I cannot remember a single time during the twenty-odd years we were privileged to entertain him when he did not forget something important. Sometimes vital medication which would necessitate an emergency visit to my doctor, but usually an essential article of clothing, particularly when we were going to a dinner dance. One year he proudly announced nothing had been forgotten, and then pandemonium broke out when he tried to get into his evening dress suit, as he had brought an old outfit not worn for some fifteen years which had been hanging in his wardrobe.

It was now several sizes too small, and trying to fit him into this and covering up the gaps around his middle with an old cummerbund belonging to my husband, was a most hilarious experience.

One of the most famous stories which Albert told and which no doubt many of his friends have heard, was when he decided to varnish his lavatory seat on Saturday evening. Early Sunday morning he visited the toilet, totally forgetting the condition of the seat, and needless to say he stuck to it! He managed to alert his neighbours who called for help, and he was finally taken to hospital with a blanket wrapped around both Albert and the seat! Lying face downwards on a bed in a casualty ward, he remarked to the young doctor in attendance, 'I bet you have never seen one of these before,' to which the doctor replied, 'On the contrary, Mr Best, I have seen many, but never before in a frame!' The list of funny incidents is endless, and I am sure his friends could compile a book of humorous happenings to Albert. Albert loved to be with his friends on social occasions and have a good gossip, but he was never malicious. His powers of exaggeration were excellent, and I told him frequently that his small goldfish became large salmon when he had repeated the story a number of times.

Albert had another totally different side to his character. Proud, independent, and in many ways a lonely man. He was very modest, realising he had a very special gift from Spirit which he treated with great respect and would never abuse in any way. He set and expected a very high standard of Spirit communication and integrity from himself and other mediums and was very disturbed and angry when he witnessed a lack of truth and sincerity in another person's work. At the same time, he was always happy to help and encourage those who were entering into the field of mediumship provided they were honest and serious in their desire to be used by Spirit.

Albert always maintained he was no speaker, and preferred someone more qualified to give an address when he was taking a Church Service, but people loved listening to his anecdotes of other wonderful mediums he had known, and his sincerity always shone through.

His favourite Service was the Devotional Sunday morning at The London Spiritual Mission taken by Nan Mackenzie, and he was always happy to be staying with us when one of these Services took place. He loved this remarkable old lady and was very honoured when she asked on one occasion if he would give her a sitting, as she had not sat with another medium for very many years. After the sitting, which was given in deep trance, Albert was about to speak to Nan when he saw her guide Running Water standing beside her, in full Red Indian regalia. He then realised that Nan was in trance, and Running Water proceeded to talk in a deep voice to Albert about his family and his work for Spirit for some fifteen minutes. Albert was completely overwhelmed and filled with joy and he greatly treasured that incident.

Although he had quickly switched on the recording machine, to his disappointment nothing came on the tape, but the machine had been working as Nan asked me to listen to her sitting which was really outstanding and made her so happy.

Two very great characters.

12
Au Revoir, My Friend

How fortunate I have been to have this unique and special friendship with Albert. Living so far apart his visits to our home were limited each year, but what a joy the telephone can be. Rarely a week went by when he was at home in Scotland, without several lengthy telephone calls – sometimes humorous, occasionally sad, often gossipy, sometimes indignant when he thought some people treated Spiritualism in an undignified manner.

It was always a joy to have him with us, talking endlessly about so many subjects, and relishing the odd glass of scotch (the latter only being partaken of at the end of the day when all work was done). Albert called our friendship unconditional, and I treasure the little plaque he gave me at one time, telling me "This refers to us, Ros."

"Friendship is the comfort, the inexpressible comfort of feeling safe with a person, having neither to weigh thoughts nor measure words, but pouring all right out just as they are, chaff and grain together, certain that a faithful friendly hand will take and sift them, keep what is worth keeping and with a breath of comfort, blow the rest away."

I still miss his physical presence and his cheery voice, but my sadness is mitigated by visualising the tremendous joy he must feel at being united with his beloved wife and children.

Until we meet again, my dear friend - *Slainte Mhath*, Albert (pronounced Slanji Va).

13

Exit

Gordon Smith writes:

"Since knowing Albert Best I have seen and heard many phenomenal things, but being with him and seeing that wonderful expression on his face when he saw his beloved wife and children appear to him was indeed the most special experience that I can recall, especially as Albert himself had benefitted from this truly special spiritual experience. I do feel that it is fitting to share this story with others who would wish to learn about this great man. Albert Best has been a great influence in my life, not only as a brilliant medium but also as a true friend. He once said of me that I had the potential to become a fine medium. I hope one day to repay Albert by fulfilling this potential he has seen in me.

Ann, Jim and Gordon, our Last Visit with Albert.

Albert Best was taken into hospital on 2nd April 1996. Shortly after being admitted Albert slipped into a coma from which he never regained full consciousness.

On the evening of Thursday 11th April Ann Docherty, Jim McManus and I were the last people visiting that evening. We were told that the visit was over but the nurse in charge asked if we would like to spend some extra time with Albert. Ann was standing at the right-hand side of the bed. She had one hand on Albert's forehead. I was beside Ann and was holding his right hand. Jim faced me and was holding Albert's left hand. We stood in silence, all of us looking at him. I remember thinking that

Albert was in the best hands, as both Ann and Jim are very good spiritual healers and of course we all cared. Just at that moment I became aware of a presence at the foot of the bed. I turned my head but of course no one was physically standing there. I looked to Ann and then to Jim to see if either of them had felt as I did but it seemed to me that they hadn't. As I looked down on him I could see that he had begun to stir. Mentally I spoke to him, trying to encourage him to open his eyes, there seemed to be an energy build-up at the bottom of the bed. Only this time I could not turn my head, instead I focused my gaze on Albert. In that moment he opened his eyes, turned his head to Jim and smiled, then to me, finally he looked up at Ann and tried to speak. None of us could make out what he had tried to say that time. However, he repeated the statement and this time we definitely did understand.

He said 'My wife is here and the children,' his eyes turned to face the foot of the bed and his eyes opened wide, he smiled and lifted his head. His smile became brighter, in my mind's eye I could visualise a young lady standing there, slim build with long auburn hair. Albert was transfixed. As I looked to Jim I could see clearly that he had a lump in his throat and Ann had tears running down her cheeks and I could feel the tears welling up in my eyes. His gaze went round the three of us standing there then he spoke his last words when he said 'They've come. You will have to let me go.'

Ann replied 'We were never holding you, Albert.'

He gave us one last smile and then lowered his head gently to the pillow and closed his eyes. Albert remained in the coma until he took his transition the following evening, Friday 12th April. I will always remember the words that the doctor attending Albert said to me 'This very special man has just gone home. God bless, Mr Best.'

To Albert – Ann, Jim and I wish you great joy which is no more than you deserve."

Lightning Source UK Ltd.
Milton Keynes UK
UKHW021315210120
357348UK00008B/1422